Interplay of Domestic Politics and Foreign-Security Policy of Iran

Interplay of Domestic Politics and Foreign-Security Policy of Iran

By

Dr. Shah Alam

Vij Books India Pvt Ltd
New Delhi (India)

Published by

Vij Books India Pvt Ltd
(Publishers, Distributors & Importers)
2/19, Ansari Road
Delhi – 110 002
Phones: 91-11-43596460, 91-11-47340674
Fax: 91-11-47340674
e-mail: vijbooks@rediffmail.com

The views expressed in the book are of author in his personal capacity.

Contents

Preface

The Revolution of 1979 completely transformed Iran, domestic situation changed, and religion coalesced with politics. The fusion of religion and politics had profound impact within Iran, and transformed Iran's polity, society, and economy. The Revolution replaced monarchy with the clerics-rule. As domestic situation changed, it also set about changes in foreign and security policy of the Islamic Republic. A close relationship was built between domestic politics and foreign-security policy in 1979, which still continues. This relationship between domestic politics and foreign-security policy has corresponding effects within Iran and beyond.

Ayatollah Khomeini transformed Iran in many ways. He not only changed the domestic situation, but also its foreign and security policy. Iran reversed the Shah regime's policies, and ruptured relations with the outside world. The Islamic Republic defined and redefined its security policy as departed from the western security camp. As Iran departed from the western security camp, following the Revolution, the context and connotation of security changed. It built its security apparatus along Islamic line as appears from the formations of ideological forces and indoctrination of the armed forces. It illustrates from the Islamic Republic's words and deeds and theory and practice that domestic situation has profound impact over foreign and security policy. Domestic politics and foreign-security policy have a close relationship and are complex as well.

Ayatollah Khomeini had pursued a different style of diplomacy. The Islamic Republic introduced 'Neither East Nor West' as a foreign policy approach. Initially, Iran took hard stance on the issue of relations with the outside world, but later softened its attitude towards the east, and opened relations with selected countries. Iran's trade with the outside world affected as a result of its regional and global isolation. Iran's external trade declined as it ruptured ties with the outside world. It had negligible trade with the West in the 1980s. The Iran-Iraq War ceasefire in July 1988 paved the way for improvement in relations with the outside world. Iran's relations with the outside world began to improve, but could not maintain it to the level of pre-Revolution period due to varieties of reasons.

The demise of Ayatollah Khomeini on 3 June 1989 and change in leadership paved the way in improving Iran's relations with the outside world. Iranian leadership sought to recover economy which was shattered during eight years of war with Iraq. Iran sought engagement with the outside world to recover economy with foreign technology and capital. So, President Hashemi Rafsanjani sent conciliatory messages to the world, and pursued rapprochement policy. Iran expressed desire to engage with the world and integrate into it. The action of the West and the United State discouraged the Iranians and added animosity in Iran's relations with the West and the US. President Bill Clinton pursued 'Dual Containment Policy' (Iran and Iraq) in 1992, which did not go well within Iran. The US imposed sanctions against Iran in the mid-1990s that further discouraged and alienated the Iranians. Iranian domestic situation was also changing due to growth and activities of political factions.

Iran's domestic situation began to change in the absence of Ayatollah Khomeini and various political factions increased their activities. The growth and activities of various political factions were curtailed in the 1980s, in the name of security, since Iran was on war with Iraq. The growing activities of the political factions in the 1990s did not only affect domestic politics but also foreign and security policy. Factional politics in the mid-1990s intensified and took clear shape by the end of 1996. Political polarisation intensified, the Moderates-Reformists Islamists gained popularity, consolidated their position, and won the May 1997 presidential elections. Iran's polity was so polarised in 1997 that it vertically split into two blocs – the Conservatives-Radicals and the Moderates-Reformists; and gave birth to a bi-polar polity in Iran. The effects of political divisions appeared at Iran's foreign and security policy as illustrated in Khatami's pursuit of policies.

Mohammad Khatami made endeavours to improve Iran's relations with the foreign countries and adopted measures. He improved Iran's relations with the regional countries such as the Gulf countries and Saudi Arabia. Iran's relations with the eastern countries improved during his presidency as well. Khatami could not improve Iran's relations with the US and enmity between the two countries continued. Domestic political situation was also changing due to Khatami's desire of political and social reforms at home. Alarm bell rung in the Conservatives-Radicals as President Khatami introduced changes in Iran's polity and society. The Conservatives-Radicals disliked Khatami's foreign and security policy too. Alignment and realignment began and consolidation of the conservatives solidified. Political factions reorganised, and polarisation intensified in 2004. The Conservatives-Radicals garnered supports in their favour, contested the June 2005 presidential elections, and came out victorious.

Mahmoud Ahmedinejad won the June 2005 presidential elections and reversed Khatami's policies. This impact of political divisions was witnessed in pursuit of Ahmedinejad's policies, adopted during his presidency. President Ahmedinejad pursued a different style of diplomacy and its expressions appeared in Iran's posture in the 1980s. Ahmedinejad's confrontational policy led Iran towards regional and global isolation. Iran's isolation and sanctions one after another adversely affected Iran's economy and trade. Iranian economy suffered due to economic sanctions and people faced economic hardship. The popularity of the Conservatives-Radicals gradually declined and political alignment and realignment began. The Moderates-Reformists gradually consolidated and gained popularity. The growing popularity of the Moderates-Reformists and their consolidation rose expectations to win the June 2013 presidential elections.

Hassan Rouhani got support of the Moderates-Reformists and won the June 2013 presidential elections, even though he belonged to the conservatives. He was considered as a moderate by the Moderates-Reformists and they extended support to Rouhani in order to halt the conservatives hardliner's prospect for wining the June 2013 presidential elections. President Rouhani pursued 'engagement policy' in his foreign and security policy approach as well as in the domestic policy. President Rouhani with the consent of Ayatollah Khamenei started negotiations with the P-5 +1 (US, Britain, France, Russia, and China + Germany) on Iran's nuclear programme and reached an agreement on 14 July 2015 which was halted during Ahmedinejad presidency. It appears that President Rouhani has brought changes in the realm of security policy. Iran's foreign policy also witnesses changes.

Domestic situation and foreign-security policy continue to enjoy close relationship which began in 1979. Iran's words and deeds and theory and practice illustrate that domestic politics and foreign-security policy have close relationship. As domestic situation changed, Iran's foreign and security policy too changed. As illustrated from Ayatollah Khomeini to Hassan Rouhani, Iran's foreign and security policy is virtually a mirror image of its 'domestic politics'.

My indebtedness to numerous persons and institutions is in fact much more than I may really express in words, yet I would attempt to do so in my most humble way. First of all, I owe my sincere gratitude to my supervisor Dr. M. H. Ilias for his keen interest and scholarly guidance.

My special thanks to Prof. Sujit Dutta and Prof. Gulshan Dietl for their suggestions at various stages of writing this study and their help in all possible ways to complete it. I would also like to thank Prof. Jawaid Ahmed Khan and Dr. Sameena for their cooperation.

This work is a Post-Doctoral Fellowship, which is sponsored by the Indian Council of Social Science Research (ICSSR), New Delhi. The ICSSR has assisted financially and always extended its cooperation in smooth conduct of this study. I extend my heartiest thanks especially to Director, Senor Fellowship Division (SRF Division), Dr. Sanchita Dutta, and her staff for their help and cooperation in completing this study. I also thank all other ICSSR staff for their cooperation and help at all stages.

Without the courteous assistance of the staff of the libraries of Jamia Millia Islamia (JMI), Jawaharlal Nehru University (JNU), A. M. U Aligarh, Institute for Defence Studies and Analysis (IDSA), the British Council, the American Culture, Sapru House, and Iranian Cultural House, this study could not have been completed. I duly acknowledge their help, and thank all of them.

— **Shah Alam**

Chapter - 1

Introduction

Religious, liberals, leftists, intelligentsia and workers participated in demonstrations, protests, and strikes in 1978-79 that culminated into revolution. It was a coalition of diverse forces under leadership of Ayatollah Khomeini that turned Iran into a new phase. Religious symbols were used to mobilise the masses against the Shah since the regime could not ban it. Mosques were used for gatherings and meetings which turned into political activities. The coalition forces opposed the Shah, but did not have any specific and clear agenda for the post-Shah Iran. Religion played a dominant role during the Revolution and overshadowed everything. The 1979 Revolution was a long process of political socialisation which overthrew the Shah and transformed Iran's society, polity, foreign policy, security, and economy.

The dominance of religion during the Revolution, left an indelible mark on Iran's society, polity, economy, foreign policy, and security. Religion's dominance continued in the post-Shah period that shaped political process and evolved polity in the post-Revolution Iran. With the Shah's departure, a new political culture emerged under influence of religion that swayed the political process. The emergence of a new political culture in the post-Shah period influenced the political process, which gave birth to a new political system. The new political system in the post-Revolution Iran determined its state behaviour. The event of 1979 did not only change Iran's domestic politics, but also its foreign policy. As Iran's foreign policy changed in the post-Shah period, security came under stress, and required a new definition. The concept of security was defined and redefined since Iran had departed from the western security camp. As Iran departed from the western security camp, it had to rely on its own resources to ensure security, and so religion was employed in forces formations.

As the Revolution of 1979 changed domestic politics, Iran's foreign policy too underwent major changes. Ayatollah Khomeini completely reversed the previous regime's foreign policy orientations and objectives that had evolved over a period of time. Iran snapped ties with the world in order to become 'independent' since the Shah regime was depicted during the Revolution as dependent on the US and the West by the revolutionaries. Iran's revisionist foreign policy created bitterness in the region and beyond, and deteriorated its relations with outside world. Meanwhile Iran-Iraq war further complicated the domestic situation and Iran sought to ensure its security and territorial integrity. A friendless Iran sought to ensure its territorial integrity and security, defined and redefined the concept of security to ward off threats.

Domestic situation played vital role in determining foreign and security policy following the Revolution since the new regime concentrated its efforts to ensure its survival. The Revolution 1979 broke the status quo within Iran that worried the regional countries, the US, and the West. For the regional countries, their survival seemed at stake. For the United States and the West, their interests in the region and beyond perceived to be threatened. For the new regime in Iran, its survival perceived to be threatened. Some countries in the region, the US, and the West wished to dislodge the new regime of Iran and made concerted efforts in this direction, but in vain. As they made efforts to dislodge the regime in Iran, they inadvertently strengthened the regime, and Iran survived. External players' role domestically strengthened the hands of new leadership, Ayatollah Khomeini, in consolidating power.

However, Iran delved into isolation following the revolution since it had broke its ties with the outside world in order to become independent. Islamisation process in Iran was perceived as threat among the regional countries and beyond. Iran's revolutionary slogans such as 'Export of Revolution' made it friendless in the region and beyond. Religion played major role in setting direction of domestic politics, thus swayed the foreign and security policy of Iran.

With the Iran-Iraq War ceasefire in July 1988, Iran's relations with outside world began to improve. The normalisation process in Iran's external relations began and the European countries started to lift economic and political sanctions against Iran. The demise of Ayatollah Khomeini in June 1989 and new leadership at Tehran accentuated in normalisation process of Iran's external relations. As the domestic political situation changed, Iran's behaviour with the outside world appeared shifted. The change appeared in the late 1980s and followed into the 1990s, but could not normalise its relations with the US and the West as expected due to several reasons. Hashemi Rafsanjani made efforts to normalise Iran's relations with the outside world but the US policy towards Iran became a hurdle in this direction. The US and the West imposed sanctions in the mid-1990s that became main obstacles in normalising Iran's relations with the outside world. But the presidential elections result of the May 1997 raised expectations for a change in Iran's foreign and security policy.

The result of the May 1997 presidential elections raised expectations for improvement in Iran's relations with the outside world. Mohammad Khatami (1997-2005) made efforts to increase Iran's acceptability in the world and expanded relations with outside world which was initiated by his predecessor, Hashemi Rafsanjani. As he started to improve relations with the outside world, the forces within Iran became active, and domestic politics appeared change. The groups/factions began to organise and reorganise against the Moderates-Reformists and resisted Khatami's policy. The grouping around the Conservatives-Radicals dented Khatami's efforts and his policies. However, Mohammad Khatami's efforts yielded some tangible results and could improve Iran's relations with the outside world. The result of the June 2005 presidential election changed the domestic situation and the Conservatives-Radicals ascended to power.

Mahmoud Ahmedinejad won the June 2005 presidential elections by defeating heavy weight politician Hashemi Rafsanjani. Ahmedinejad reversed policies of the previous regime and assertion appeared in Iran's foreign and security policy. He pursued a pro-active regional policy and opened uranium enrichment process that was suspended voluntarily and temporarily by Mohammad Khatami in negotiations of October 2003 and November 2004 with the E-3 (Britain, France, and Germany). Thus, assertion in Iran's foreign and security policy appeared the same as regime changed at Tehran. The Conservatives-Radicals continued policies which isolated Iran internationally. The UN, the US, and the European countries imposed sanctions one after another and Iranian economy suffered. Iran's international isolation left adverse impact over its economy, thus domestic situation also started to change. By 2012, the conservatives divided and domestic political alignment and realignment began. As division within the conservatives appeared the Moderates-Reformists Islamists took advantages of the opportunity. The Moderates-Reformists united and extended support to Hassan Rouhani in the June 2013 presidential elections, they considered him a moderate. In the June 2013 presidential elections, Hassan Rouhani got support of the Moderates-Reformists and Rafsanjani faction, and won.

The division within the conservatives, alignment of Moderates-Reformists forces, and support of Rafsanjani faction became the main factors in defeating the conservatives candidates by Hassan Rouhani. Although Rouhani belongs to the conservatives side, but now is considered as moderate. With election of Hassan Rouhani as president in June 2013 appeared changes in Iran's foreign and security policy. Undoubtedly, as domestic situation witnessed changes, Iran's foreign and security policy takes shift. From Ayatollah Khomeini to Hassan Rouhani shift witnessed changes in Iran's foreign and security policy.

Undoubtedly, the dominant position of the *Velayat-e Faqih* in Iran's political system has left a little space for the president to act independently. The *Velayat-e Faqih* is one of the most important institutions in Iran which carries vast powers and functions. Thus, Ayatollah Khamenei has vast powers and functions in Iranian system similar to Ayatollah Khomeini. This institution plays vital roles in determining foreign and security policy despite directly elected presidency. President plays a role in determining foreign and security policy, but vital and major role is being played by the *Velayat-e Faqih*. But the *Velayat-e Faqih* is also influenced with domestic political dynamics and changing factional alliances.

The Concept

Relationship between domestic politics and foreign-security policy of Iran continues to exist since the Revolution of 1979. The effects of domestic developments over Iran's foreign-security policy have appeared throughout the post-Revolution Iran. Domestic situation has been playing decisive role in formulation and implementation of foreign and security policy and they have close relationship.[1] Ayatollah Khomeini led the masses against the Shah, overthrew monarchy and established clerics-rule in Iran. With establishment of clerics-rule in Iran, impact was reflected over Iran's foreign and security policy. Religion played a decisive role in overthrowing monarchy, and the post-monarchy era witnessed religious influence over political process of Iran. Political process started following the Revolution, dominance of religion appeared in all aspects. As a religion, Islam is all encompassing, regulating almost every aspect of life and domestic politics, including foreign, defence, and security policy of Iran.[2] Thus, domestic situation is the principal factor in determining foreign and security policy in the post-Revolution Iran. The Islamic Republic ruptured relations with outside world in order to become independent since the clerics-rule regime perceived interactions with outside world as threat to the regime and the country.

Relations between domestic politics and foreign-security policy of Iran has been consistently and persistently seen since the 1979 Revolution. As new administration installs at Tehran, changes appear in foreign and security policy. Undoubtedly, the close relationship between domestic situation and foreign-security policy, which appeared in the early 1980s, continues to exist. The changes in nature, kind, orientation, and objective of Iranian policy appeared in the post-Revolution period linked to domestic situations. The shifts in domestic politics appeared as political factions/groups grew and increased their activities. The effects of these political factions/groups activities were witnessed in Iran's polity, foreign policy, defence policy, and security policy.[3] Thus, domestic situation and the changing character of Iranian polity have had deep impact over Iran's foreign and security policy.

This study raises the questions such as; what is the relationship between domestic situation and foreign-security policy of Iran and how has domestic politics remained the principal factor in determining Iran's foreign and security policy and vice versa? How have political factions/groups' growth and their activities affected Iran's polity? How has evolving polity of Iran affected foreign and security policy? Has the changing character of Iran's polity affected foreign and security policy? Has the changing Iran's polity affected political culture? Has the changing strategic culture, affected foreign and security policy of Iran? How have changes appeared at foreign and security policy since the new Administration was installed at Tehran? How has foreign issues and foreign powers affected Iran's domestic politics. Are the foreign issues and foreign powers remained significant points in deciding Iran's domestic politics and country's behaviour? Political developments inside Iran have effects over its external behaviour.

The relationship between domestic politics and foreign-security policy has continued since 1979 as reflects from the Islamic Republic's policies. The leader of Iranian Revolution, Ayatollah Khomeini brought changes which affected the whole Iran. Each Administration tried to bring changes in the post-Khomeini period, but could not alter the political system as evolved during the Khomeini period. In the post-Khomeini period, Ayatollah Khamenei is principal arbiter pertaining to polity, foreign policy, defence policy, and security policy as his predecessor. Iran experienced changes in foreign and security policy in the post-Khomeini period, but also witnessed continuity, and could not delink from previous policies because of domestic factors. In the absence of Ayatollah Khomeini, Ayatollah Khamenei has been playing principal role in shaping domestic politics, foreign policy, defence policy, and security policy. As a result, continuity with change has been seen at Iran's domestic politics, foreign and security policy, and defence policy.

Literature Survey

Iranian polity has been consistently and persistently affected by factionalism, and as a result, has affected foreign and security policy. Iran's domestic situation has been consistently influencing foreign and security policy. The relationship between domestic politics and foreign-security policy of Iran developed in the early 1980s, still continues. Substantial works have not yet been done on this subject and it deserves to receive attention. Except two books, works that focus on factional politics and its impact over forming policies in the post-Revolution Iran, there are only a few articles in some journals. The articles are generally descriptive and discuss views of the factions and who belongs to what faction. The factions/groups affect political configurations, consequently influence policy issues including foreign and security policy. Shahrough Akhavi's work "Elite Factionalism in the Islamic Republic of Iran" (1987) explains that the elite had successfully consolidated its power, but had failed to evolve consistent public policies, a consistency which normally attends power consolidation.[4] He analyses that inconsistencies in policies persisted because of revolutionary conditions and the Iran-Iraq War. Internal conflict within the ruling elite prevented, for some areas, the articulation of policy lines even on paper.[5] The political system is centralised around the *Velayat-e Faqih* and the key judicial institutions. The contention between factions on socio-economic issues seemed quite strong but the clerics were united on cultural issues: education, nationalities policy, and the role of women following the Revolution. Divisions among elites appeared on foreign policy issues. Akhavi points out that Hussein Ali Muntaziri and Ali Akbar Hashemi Rafsanjani sought to restore relations with the United States in the 1984-1986 period but Hujjat al-Islam Ali Khamenei (Iran's current *Velayat-e Faqih*), Ayatollah Ali Mishkini (then Chairman of the Council of Experts and Friday mosque prayer leader of Qum), Hujjat al-Islam Khu'ayniha (then State Prosecutor General), Mir Hussein Mussavi (two-term Prime Minister), and others opposed.[6] As divisions in political elites on policy issues appeared in the 1980s that still persists.

Maziar Behrooz's paper "Factionalism in Iran under Khomeini" (1991) describes factions and their views on various issues during Khomeini.[7] Behrooz concurs with Akhavi and explains that factions/groups contested on social, political, foreign policy, and economic issues and factions struggled to influence policy issues. The factions/groups such as "conservatives", "radicals", and "moderates" existed during Ayatollah Khomeini. But Ayatollah Khomeini normally avoided in siding with particular factions or groups. Ayatollah Khomeini had preferred to remain aloof from conflicts of the elite prior to 1987 and interfered only on rare occasions when the situation was about to get out of control. While Ayatollah Khomeini was the ultimate authority, factions sought his approval for their legitimacy, and played an important role in shaping his own views. Behrooz viewed that the Iran-Iraq War ceasefire in July 1988 added a new dimension to, and intensified, factional conflicts.[8] The end of the Iran-Iraq War in 1988 introduced, or rather injected, Iran's foreign policy as an important source of clashes between the factions/political groups.[9] But Behrooz disagrees with Akhavi on the issue of foreign policy during Khomeini period. Iran's priorities during the Iran-Iraq War were different and foreign policy remained, for the most part, outside factional struggle. Sudden end of the Iran-Iraq War changed domestic situation rapidly and made foreign policy an important issue in factional struggles.[10] The factional struggles over Iran's foreign policy had continued between 1979 and 1988, but remained low. After Iran-Iraq War ceasefire, the Radicals clashed with the Moderates over foreign policy and reconstruction. The factional struggles continued over Iran's foreign policy and economic reconstruction and intensified in 1990 and later.[11] The tussle between the Radicals and Moderates over socio-political, economic, and foreign policy issues continued after Khomeini's demise in June 1989.

Factionalism continued in the Post-Khomeini period that affected decision making in Iran. Nader Entessar's work "Factional Politics in Post-Khomeini Iran: Domestic and Foreign Policy Implications" (1994) is an analysis of factional politics after Ayatollah Khomeini and its impact over Iran's foreign policy.[12] He distinguishes among three factions within the elite – the Pragmatists, the Conservatives, and the Radicals. The persistence of multiple centres of power and factionalism within ruling groups have resulted in discussions and debates over socio-political and economic issues in Iran. The existence of acute factionalism has led to paralyses in decision making on political, economic, and foreign policy issues.[13] In Entessar's view, foreign policy has been arena of debates among the factions and they influence in shaping Iran's relations with the outside world.

Factional struggles continued over Iran's foreign policy and security policy in the post-Khomeini period. The Conservatives-Radicals and the Moderates-Reformists clashed over Iran's foreign policy and security issues. Masoud Kazemzadeh's work "Intra-Elite Factionalism and the 2004 Majles Elections in Iran" (2008) offers to understand factional divisions over important issues including foreign and security policy. He says that the Conservatives-Radicals view the United States and Israel as hostile and this faction seeks to increase relations with Russia, China, and North Korea.[14] Kazemzadeh states factional divisions over security issues like Iran's nuclear policy. The paper explicitly illustrates deep divisions between the Conservatives-Radicals and the Moderates-Reformists over Iran's foreign policy and security issues including nuclear programme during Khatami period. The Conservatives-Radicals advocate for continued nuclear programme, withdrawal from the Nuclear Non-proliferation Treaty (NPT), and expulsion of the International Atomic Energy Agency (IAEA) from Iran.[15] Kazemzadeh analyses deep divisions among factions on Iran's domestic issues as well as foreign policy and security issues.

Bahman Baktiari's paper "Iran's Conservative Revival" (2007) explains revival of the conservatives and their positions on Iran's foreign and security policy including economic issues.[16] Baktiari agrees with Kazemzadeh on political divisions in Iran over foreign policy and security issues. He says the Moderates like Hashemi Rafsanjani seek to restore relations with the United States, but the Conservatives-Radicals are against it. Baktiari explains assertion of the conservative factions on Iran's foreign and security policy that appeared after victory of conservative hardliner Mahmoud Ahmedinejad in the June 2005 presidential elections. Baktiari analyses the conservative hardliner Ahmedinejad's election as president in 2005 heralded assertion in Iran's positions regarding foreign policy, and nuclear programmes.[17] The political factions/groups are clearly divided over Iran's security issues including nuclear programme.

The work of Mehran Kamrava "Iranian National Security Debates: Factionalism and Lost Opportunities" (2007) discusses factions and their views on national security issues in the post-Revolution Iran.[18] Kamrava analyses factions and shifting alliances that make Iranian polity highly fluid. It illustrates political dynamics and fluid nature of factions in Iran. It is an analysis of positions and views of factions on Iran's national security issues including foreign policy. As the factions shift their alliances, changes appear in their views and positions on the issues. Kamrava says that Iran has pursued incoherent national security policy due to shifting factional alliances and their positions on issues.[19] The shifting factional alliances have affected decision making process.

Ideological divisions among the Iranian elite remained in the early days of the Revolution and faction/groups disagreed on key issues and policies. Mehdi Moslem's book *Factional Politics in Post-Khomeini Iran* traces Iran's factional politics, its roots, dynamics and ideological differences both the Khomeini period and after. It offers an overall view of factions and discusses how the existence of factions/groups prevents Iran from forming coherent domestic, foreign, and security policies.[20] While Khomeini was alive, any ideological tension due to these differences was, by and large, diffused through his interventions. Since Khomeini's demise in June 1989, these differences have both solidified and intensified and the ideological discord among the ruling elite has become the most salient feature of politics in Iran. Iranian polity is composed of ideological blocs and each bloc shares and advances its own particular interpretation of issues and policies. Moslem classifies factions as groups, organisations, classes, and clergy as well as non-clergy, who disagree on the nature and character of the theocracy's political system and its policies in different spheres.[21] Each faction/group seeks to promote and advance its own policies. Lack of ideological cohesion and clear direction has adversely affected Iran in all areas of policy making.[22] As the title indicates, the book does not place foreign and security policy at the centre of its analysis. It is primarily an analysis of factions and factional politics in post-Khomeini Iran and examines views and positions of various factions on different issues. It treats foreign and security policy as one of its dimensions.

Anoushirvan Ehteshami and Mahjoob Zweiri's book *Iran and the Rise of its Neoconservatives: The Politics of Tehran's Silent Revolution* offers to understand how Ahmedinejad emerged to champion the Right faction (Radical faction) and what his electoral success has meant for the traditionalists, conservatives, and reformers alike.[23] The work discusses systemic problems that Iran's political system is based on a number of competing institutions – *the Majlis*, presidency, the ministries, the judiciary, the Expediency Council, the Guardian Council, and the *Velayat-e Faqih*. The book analyses revival of the Conservatives-Radicals and its impact over policy issues. Ehteshami and Zweiri assume "future power contestation" is to emerge between the old faction of the conservatives and the new guard. This work is an analysis of failure of the previous two presidencies and the rise of the Radicals within the Conservatives. As the title indicates, this book ignores foreign and security policy at the centre of its analysis.

It analyses failure of the previous administrations and examine dynamics of politics at different levels. It treats foreign and security policy as one of its aspects.

The first drawback of the literature on Iranian domestic politics is its descriptive and non-analytical nature and lack of linkages between domestic political situation and foreign-security policy. The conventional literature lacks a clear and systematic definition of factions/groups and their views on foreign and security policy of Iran. None of the publications provides clear views of factions/groups on policy issues such as foreign policy and security issues. Conventional literature largely ignores the historical roots and reasons for emergence of political factions. The current literature does not mention political trends and alignment of factions to a particular political tendency. It also ignores to analyse shifting factional alliances and its impact over policy issues such as foreign and security policy. The existing literature on domestic politics reflects on factional politics and shifts and rifts in factional alliances and balance of power – changes that have often challenged previous policies and views of the factions/groups. An important contribution of this work is its establishing linkages between domestic politics and foreign-security policy.

The conventional literatures on domestic politics and foreign-security policy neglect the role, influence, and impact of Iranian society on ideological divisions among the elite. None of the works explains political trends in the post-revolution Iran and alignment of factions to a particular political tendency. The existing works suggests that ideological divisions in Iran are not restricted only to the elite, ideological discord has permeated Iranian society as well. Society's views and interests cannot be ignored since it is an important component of both political process and factional politics in Iran. Both conventional literatures and existing works neglect analysis of political trends in Iran and factions' alignment to a particular political tendency. Finally, the literatures lack theoretical and analytical rigour.

The existing literatures also neglect to explain explicitly how and why various political factions/groups are able to force their preferences and promote their views despite existence of other factions who wish to do the same. The existing works do not explain political tendencies in the post-

Revolution Iran and each faction's alignment to a particular political trend. The existing literatures discuss policy issues, but use foreign and security policy as a reference. The current literatures fail to link domestic situation including factional politics with foreign and security policy. Such linkages are required and sin qua non.

Finally, the current literatures on domestic politics and foreign-security policy oversimplify domestic politics' relation with foreign-security policy of Iran. The existing literatures serve only as precursor for a more critical analysis of domestic politics including factions and its relation with foreign and security policy of Iran. As narratives, these works investigates domestic situation, but neglects its linkages with foreign and security policy. A major shortcoming of the literatures is its neglect of socio-economic base of the political factions/groups that affect factional alliances in Iran and compete for power in domestic politics. So, this study requires systematic, comprehensives, and critical analysis of political trends, domestic political dynamics including factional politics, alignment of factions to a particular political trend and its impact over foreign and security policy.

Methodology

This work is based on both empirical and analytical. It seeks to build an argument that explains the political changes and processes on the basis of a close scrutiny of the relevant developments and data. It justifies arguments of the study by explaining and analysing the developments, policy statements and data. Primary sources are used in the form of official statements, policies, and policy statements. Interactions with selected officials and intellectuals, and specialists are used in writing the study. Secondary sources have been also used in preparing the study.

Organisation of Book

The work has been organised systematically into chapters and each contains separate issue, and differs from others. The first chapter introduces the subject and lays out theoretical framework upon which the work is based. It discusses concept, survey of literatures, methodology, and the organisation of the study. The second chapter systematically explains and analyses domestic situation, political dynamic, political trends, factions/parties and factionalism. It discusses factions' views and positions on policy issues. This section devotes how have domestic political developments affected polity and political system? It analyses administrative changes at Tehran and policy shifts. The third chapter deals with how foreign policy of Iran changes as new administration installs at Tehran. It analyses factional alliances, their policy preferences, and changing foreign policy. This section analyses and establishes relationship between domestic politics including factional politics and foreign policy of the Islamic Regime. The effects of domestic political dynamics over foreign policy are discussed in detail. The fourth chapter explains security policy in the post-Revolution Iran and various competing institutions influence security policy. This section devotes to analyse the shifts in security policy due to administrative changes. It explains Iran's security perception, security strategy, military doctrine, formation of ideological forces and nuclear policy. This section critically analyses factional approach pertaining to security issues. The fifth chapter draws conclusion of the study and brings out effects of domestic situation in Iran on its foreign and security policy.

What is New

The study systematically explains and analyses the subject, justifies its arguments, and finally draws conclusion. Domestic situation and domestic political dynamics are principal factors in determining foreign-security policy of the Islamic Republic. Factionalism and factional politics continues to play significant role in deciding state behaviour. As the alliances form, they begin to affect the administration and consequently influence foreign and security policy. The conventional literature describes domestic politics, foreign policy, and security policy but they could not establish close linkages between domestic politics including factional politics and foreign-security policy of Iran. The existing works discusses factional politics, but neglect to establish linkages between factional politics and foreign-security policy. This study systematically explains political trends in post-Revolution Iran and alignment of factions to a particular political tendency. This work critically analyses as domestic political alliances alter, administrative changes follow and the shifts appear in foreign and security policy. The study critically analyses political factions and changing alliances in post-Revolution Iran and establishes linkages between the domestic political dynamics and foreign and security policy.

The post-Revolution Iran witnessed policy shifts as administrative changes took place. As Iran entered into a new phase its priorities and orientation changed. Ayatollah Khomeini pursued confrontational foreign policy since domestic politics demanded. Ayatollah Khomeini's management style had left indelible mark on polity and foreign-security policy of Iran. In the absence of Ayatollah Khomeini, the new leadership brought shifts in domestic policies and foreign policy as well. In the post-Khomeini period, as domestic politics changed, in Iran's foreign and security policy appeared shifts too. Nonetheless, Iran's Supreme Leader Ayatollah Khamenei has been playing balancing act in Iran's polity as was being done by Ayatollah Khomeini.

Undoubtedly, the process of policy formulation and decision-making in Iran is very complicated. It is a fact that the Supreme Leader Ayatollah Khamenei has the final word, but several institutions and top officials also play their role in deciding policies. The president, the heads of the *Majlis* and judicial branches, a number of ministers, military leaders, officials, and others play their role. Nonetheless, Ayatollah Khamenei is the final arbiter pertaining to polity, economy, foreign policy, and defence and security policy, but he is also influenced with domestic situation.

Rafsanjani, Khatami, and Ahmedinejad presidencies witnessed shifts in foreign and security policy approach. Each administration changed priorities and brought changes at foreign and security policy. The Rouhani Administration has been pursuing a different kind of diplomacy from Ahmedinejad as appears. President Rouhani seeks interaction and engagement with the outside world and pursues policy accordingly. The changes in President Rouhani's policy have been appearing since domestic political composition, alliances, and support base have changed. This study critically analyses effects of political dynamics and shifting alliances over foreign-security policy, whereas the existing studies ignore to provide close relationship between them.

Finally, this work is an analysis of domestic situation including factions and factional politics since 1979 and its relationship with foreign and security policy. It analysis political tendencies in the post-Revolution Iran and examines alignment of factions to a particular trend and their preferences and policy choices. It examines changing factional alliances in the post-Revolution Iran and its effects over foreign and security policy as previous works fail to establish. This study primarily focuses factional alliances and factions' positions and preferences pertaining to foreign and security policy in the post-Revolution Iran. As such this work entirely differs with previous works.

Endnotes

1 R K Ramazani, "Iran: Burying The Hatchet", *Foreign Policy*, no. 60, Fall 1985, pp. 52-74

2 Kamran Taremi, "Iranian Strategic Culture: The Impact of Ayatollah Khomeini's Interpretation of Islam", *Contemporary Security Policy*, vol. 35, no. 1, pp. 3-25

3 Mehdi Moslem, *Factional Politics in Post-Khomeini Iran* (New York: Syracuse University Press, 2002)

4 Shahrough Akhavi, "Elite Factionalism In The Islamic Republic Of Iran", *Middle East Journal*, vol. 41, no. 2, Spring 1987, P. 182.

5 Ibid.,

6 Ibid., p. 201.

7 Maziar Behrooz, "Factionalism in Iran under Khomeini", *Middle Eastern Studies*, vol. 27, no. 4, October 1991.

8 Ibid., p. 597.

9 Ibid.,

10 Ibid., p. 598.

11 Ibid., pp. 597-598

12 Nader Entessar, "Factional Politics in Post-Khomeini Iran: Domestic and Foreign Policy Implications", *Journal of South Asian and Middle Eastern Studies*, vol. 17, no. 4, Summer 1994, pp. 21-43

13 Ibid., p. 22

14 Masoud Kazemzadeh, "Intra-Elite Factionalism and the 2004 Majlis Elections in Iran", *Middle Eastern Studies*, vol. 44, no. 2, March 2008, p. 198.

15 Ibid.,

16 Bahman Baktiari, "Iran's Conservative Revival", *Current History*, vol. 106, no. 696, January 2007

17 Ibid., p. 14

18 Mehran Kamrava, "Iranian National-Security Debates: Factionalism and Lost Opportunities", *Middle East Policy*, vol. 14, no. 2, Summer 2007

19 Ibid., pp. 84- 100.

20 Moslem, n. 3, pp. 1-366

21 Ibid., p. 2

22 Ibid., pp. 3-5

23 Anoushiravan Ehteshami and Mahjoob Zweiri, *Iran and the Rise of its Neoconservatives: The Politics of Tehran's Silent Revolution* (New York: I. B. Tauris, 2007)

Chapter -2

Factional Politics

In the course of Revolution the domination of religious forces left little space for the creation of a one-party state or the emergence of independent political organisations, despite the fact that one of the main slogans of the 1979 Revolution was 'freedom'. With overthrow of Shah, a new political culture ensued that shaped the nature and character of Iranian polity. The emergency of a new political culture in 1979 was a long process of political socialisation that gave birth to a new kind of political system. With inception of new political system, domestic politics appeared changed in the post-Shah period. Political system faced challenges from domestic political dynamics and changing nature and character of Iranian polity. The dominance of religion during the 1979 Revolution overshadowed everything, however, different political tendencies continued to exist. The political tendencies contributed in shaping domestic political dynamics, thus affected policy formulation and policies of each administration.

Political process started following the Revolution and religion remained a debate among the political groups/factions. The discourse over state's nature and character started in 1979 which remained a constant debating issue among political groups/factions. The debate began in the 1980s that still continues. Iran's political system has been facing constant pressure due to domestic political dynamics. Domestic politics has remained an arena of influence of various political groups/factions despite religion's omnipresence on the entire political spectrum.

Ayatollah Khomeini's personality overshadowed the political groups/factions in the 1980s which existed in the post-Revolution Iran. All political groups/factions had struggled to influence state policy where some succeeded. However, he also took into account other political groups' views whenever and wherever required. With his demise in June 1989, new leadership took charge and Iran entered into a new phase. Iran's policy started to change as the new leadership took charge and contributed in the growth of activities of the political groups/factions. Domestic politics was completely under influence of Khomeini in the 1980s, experienced pressure from inside in his absence. The growing activities of the political groups/factions and their assertion brought pressure over political system. Thus, the assertion of political groups/factions significantly added to domestic political dynamics. Political system faced pressure due to growing activities of the various political groups/factions. These groups/factions sought to influence state's behaviour and competed with one another in determining policy issues. As a result domestic politics could not remain isolated and various political forces began to influence state's behaviour. Each successive administration brought changes in state policy that began from Hashemi Rafsanjani. Thus, domestic political developments had affected policy issues during earlier presidents, as Iran has been experiencing in the Rouhani period. However, Iran's Supreme Leader, Ayatollah Khamenei, is the final arbiter in respect to policy formulations and their implementations, and has been playing a balancing act in steering the nation.

It will firstly examine the evolution of political parties/groups in Iran and the factors which contributed to the rise of political factions/groups. Second, it will examine political trends in the post-revolution Iran. Third, the emergence of political factions/parties in the aftermath of the Revolution will be examined; and it will explain the obstacles that face political factions/parties in general, and of those which have emerged from 1997 in particular. Fourth, it will examine the political groups/factions' views on polity, economy, society, culture, security, and Iran's interaction with outside world. Fifth, it will examine the formation of coalitions/alliances by factions/groups in order to gain power and determine state behaviour. Finally, it will examine the domestic political dynamics, the emergence of bi-polar polity, and their effects over state policies and Iran's overall political system.

Evolution of Party

The Qajar dynasty (1796-1926) had witnessed unprecedented resistance from the *ulema* and *Bazaari*. Nasiruddin Shah granted the Reuter Concession 1872 to British to extract mineral resources in Iran which was protested by the *ulema* and the *Bazaari*. He further granted the Tobacco Concession 1892 to British, which was again protested by the *ulema* and the *Bazaari*. The protests continued and intensified. The continued protests by the *ulema* and the *Bazaari* forced Nassiruddin Shah to withdraw the Tobacco Concession. These two events provided opportunities to form social groups and intensify political activities. The social groups continued their movement and began to demand their representation in the government and formation of the constitution. By 1906 the three major groups, the *ulema*, the *Bazaari* and the aristocracy, formed the main pillars of the Iranian state and they became influential sources for political activities. The assassination of Nassiruddin Shah in 1896 and the Constitutional Movement 1906-11 provided fertile ground for the emergence of modern and progressive ideas, and as a result, hundreds of civil society organisations were born.

The three segments of society were not immune from sway of these predominantly middle class progressive ideas, and social and political cohesion of these groups came under pressure to open up their traditional boundaries towards modernism. The Constitutional Movement 1906-11 acted as an enlightenment trigger for Iranian politics and social thinking, forging strong roots from which current ideological trends can be traced. The new Shah, Muzafarruddin Shah Qajar (1896-1907) came under tremendous pressure as the protests for the establishment of the *Majlis* (Parliament) intensified. Under unprecedented political and social pressure, Muzaffarrudin Shah issued a decree and allowed the establishment of the *Majlis* in 1907 which was subsequently dominated by the *Hezb-e Demokrat* (the Democratic Party) and the *Hezb-e E'tedal* (the Conservative Party).[1] The First World War, the Russian Revolution 1917 and a series of other factors, sealed Iran's fragile party politics and marked the demise of the Qajar dynasty. Thus, Iran entered into a new phase, where priority was given to modernisation. Simultaneously, the activities of civil society movements became restricted as power increasingly centralised and concentrated around the new King, Reza Shah (1926-41).

By the early 1940s, Iran's political organisations were operated in traditional manners with limited numbers of members until the *Hizb-e Tudeh* (the Communist Party) and the *Jebhe-ye Milli* (the National Front Part) emerged to the forefront of the political arena. The *Hizb-e Tudeh* and *Jebhe-ye Milli* were the first two parties which opened their doors for general public and formed mass political gatherings in the 1940s and 1950s.[2] The overthrow of the Mussaddiq government in 1953 in coup froze Iran's political space for the organisations apart from three small pro-establishment parties, *Milliyum* (Nationalist), *Mardom* (the People) and the *Hezb-e Iran-e Novin* (New Iran Party). Mohammad Reza Shah Pahlavi (1941-79) decided to dissolve the *Milliyum* and the *Mardom* in favour of a new party, the *Hezb-e Rastakhiz* (the Resurgence Party) which he formed in 1975. The purpose of the regime was to strengthen political system and organise people under a political umbrella, effectively dissuading them from joining into illegal religious and Marxist organisations. However, the establishment of the *Hezb-e Rastakhiz* in 1975 significantly added to discontent.[3] The Shah's regime in 1975 destroyed even the appearance of competitive politics by creating the *Hezb-e Rastakhiz* and demanded allegiance to it. Instead of mobilising mass support for his regime, this hated party helped to provide the mass support base for the disparate socio-political forces which finally coalesced in opposition to the Shah. The Pahlavi dynasty came to an end in the 1979 Revolution. The various political trends participated during the Revolution to overthrow Mohammad Reza Shah, but they did not have a coherent policy regarding the statecraft. As a result, they continued their activities to present their ideas in shaping the post-Revolution Iran. Despite emergence of various political trends in the post-Revolution, "they never actually organised into clear-cut factions let alone into competing parties with coherent collective ideologies."[4] This feature has remained in the post-Revolution Iran's polity.

Political Trends in the Post-Revolution Iran

There are four political trends which exist in the post-Revolution. All profess and adhere an Islamic identity and display practical commitment to the principles of the constitution of the Islamic Republic. They are *Rast-e Sunnati* (the Traditional Right), *Rast-e Modern* (the Modern Right), *Chap* (the Left), and *Rast-e Efrati* (the Radical Right). The first and the fourth groups form the Conservatives-Radicals Islamists coalition, while the second and the third comprise Moderates-Reformists Islamists coalition. Each has its own social base and influences social, political, and economic spheres in Iran. Each is composed of smaller groups, publishes its own newspapers, and is supported by numerous religious and political leaders. In this way, each religious/political leader represents one of the four political trends. In the Iranian context, from the right to left this spectrum extends from social tradition, cultural conservatism, religious juridicalism, free market economics, and anti-US, anti-West and anti-Israel stances, all the way to cultural modernism, social modernism, religious liberalism, welfare-state economics, and maintaining relations with the US and the West.

The *Rast-e Sunnati* (the Traditional Right) favours free market, cultural conservatism and social traditionalism. On foreign policy, it has a conservative view. This trend seeks interactions with the foreign countries, but it should be limited and restricted. It wants limited interactions with the West, but it is sceptical to Iran's relations with the United States. In its foreign policy approach, follows 'Look East Policy'. It seeks to expand Iran's relations towards east. The *Jame'eye Ruhaniyat-e Mobarez* (JRM) (Association of the Militant Clergy of Tehran) follows this political trend. The powerful *Jame'eye Modarressin Howzeh Elmiyeye Qum* (JMHEQ) (Association of the Teachers of Qum Seminary) and *Jamiyat-e Mutalefe-e Islami* (JMI) (Islamic Coalition Society) comprise various guild and merchant groups. The JMI is dominated by the *Bazaari* (the traditional merchant class) and its members want heavy restrictions on cultural issues. The views of the *Rast-e Sunnati* are reflected in the newspapers such as *Resalat, Shoma and Farda*. The supporters of this political trend are Nateq-Nuri, Muhammad Reza Mahdavi Kani, Mohammad Yazdi, Ali Akbar Velayati, Javad Larijani, Mohammad Reza Bahonar, Murtada Nabavi, Habib Asgroladi and Abbas Ali Amid Zanjani.

The *Rast-e Modern* (Modern Right) is also called *Janah-e Miyaneh* (Modern Faction) which supports *Rast-e Sunnati* on economic matters but it advocates a more open and pragmatic approach towards cultural matters, social modernism, polity, and foreign policy. This trend advocates rapprochement with the outside world and seeks engagement with the foreign countries. It favours moderation in Iran's foreign policy approach. It advocates Iran's relations with the United States and the West. For many years *Rast-e Modern* cooperated with the *Rast-e Sunnati* and formed its own formal organisations in the early 1990s. This political trend exited during Khomeini period and acted as a political force in Iran. In the election of the Fifth *Majlis* in 1996, a section of technocrats and officials formed a group, *Khetmatgozaran-e Sazandegi* (Servants of Construction), but later on its name changed to *Kargozaran-e Sazandegi* (Executives of Construction) which had drawn many educated Iranians. Moreover, the *Rast-e Modern* has support of the *Khane-e Karegar* (House of the Workers). The newly emerging middle class supports this political trend. The supporters of this trend are former President Hashemi Rafsanjani, Gholam Hossein Karbaschi, Faezeh Rafsanjani daughter of the ex-President Hashemi Rafsanjani and Mohsen Nurbakhsh. The newspapers *Hamshahri, Iran, Akhbar, Kar Va Karegar,* and the English daily *Iran News* represent their views.

The *Chap* (Left) advocates political and cultural pluralism and its followers favour a more open political, cultural, and foreign policy spheres. This trend has conservative view on the economic issues and advocates distribution of national wealth among the people. It discourages private property ownership. In its cultural outlook, this to some extent aligned with the liberal and secular elements of society. In its foreign policy outlook, this is close to the *Rast-e Sunnati,* but differs on economic issues. It advocates moderation and engagement in Iran's foreign policy, and seeks to maintain and expand relations with the foreign countries. It favours accommodation, moderation and rapprochement in Iran's foreign policy and seeks to open relations with all countries. It advocates Iran's relations with the United States and the West. The *Chap* includes such prominent groups/sub-groups as *Daftar-e Tahkim-e Vahdat-e Howzeh va Daneshgah* (DTVHD) (the Office of Strengthening Unity between the University and the Religious Seminaries), *Anjoman-e Islami-ye Modarressin-e Daneshgahah* (AIMD) (the Society of Islamic University Teachers), *Sazman-e Mujahedin-e Enqelab-e Islami* (SMEI) (Organisation of the Mujahedin of the Islamic Revolution), *Majma-e Ruhaniyun-e Mobarez* (MRM) (Assembly of the

Combatant Clergy of Tehran, formed on 20 March 1988 by Mehdi Karrubi and Mohammad Musavi Kho'einiha), and *Jebheye Masharekat-e Iran-e Islami* (JMII) (the Front for Participation in Islamic Iran, pro-Khatami party formed in December 1998). The popular newspaper *Salam,* the bi-weekly *'Asr-e Ma,* and *Khordad* express positions of this group. The *Chap* enjoys supports of the former Prime Minister Mir-Hossein Musavi, former minister and the chief negotiator of the hostage crisis Behzad Nabavi, ex-president Mohammad Khatami, former *Majlis* Speaker Mehdi Karrubi, former Minister of Interior Hojatolislam Ali Akbar Mohtashemi-Pour, Mohammad Reza Khatami (married to Ayatollah Khomeini's granddaughter, brother to former President Mohammad Khatami), former Deputy Minister of Intelligence Saeed Hajarian (theoretician of reform movement, advisor to Mohammad Khatami), Abbas Abidi (leader students who took American diplomats hostage 1979-81, foreign ministry official thereafter), and Mohammad Salamati.

The *Rast-e Efrati* (Radical Right) believes in social conservatism, cultural conservatism, authoritarianism, curtailment of freedom of expression, distribution of national wealth (oil money and resources), and subsidies to poor. It believes in welfare-state economics. This trend favours confrontational approach in Iran's foreign policy. It does not want expansion of Iran's relations with the foreign countries. It favours limited and restricted engagements with the outside world. In its belief, Iran's interactions with the outside world would bring bad things to home, and would pollute socially and culturally to Iran. Economically, Iran will be exploited by the foreign countries. It opposes Iran's relations with the United States. It favours Iran's 'Look East Policy'. It supports in expansion of Iran's relations towards eastern countries. This trend aligns to the *Rast-e Sunnati* on social, cultural, political and foreign policy issues. The *Rast-e Efrati* is close to the *Chap* on economic issues. This political trend is subscribed by the Revolutionary Guards and *Basej*[5]. The Islamic Revolutionary Guard Corps (IRGC) founded in May 1979, has been incorporated into the state apparatus, particularly in the Ministry of Jehad for Construction, is the main state contractor. After the ceasefire of the Iran-Iraq War in 1988, the *Basej* returned to their studies and became politically more active. The former intelligence minister, Mohammad

Reyshahri founded an organisation shortly before the *Majlis* election 1996, *Jamiyat-e Defa'az Arzeshha-ye Enqlab-e Islami* (Society for the Defence of the Values of the Islamic Revolution) represents this trend. The *Ansar-e Hezbollah* (Helpers of the Party of God) believes in authoritarianism and manifests anti-intellectual positions towards culture and life-style, follows their views. The *Abadgaran-e Iran Islami* (AII) (Islamic Iran Developers) follows this political trend. This group comprises mostly young men who seek to maintain Islamic social code and break up any social gathering which is oriented against the establishment. They also organise street protests and disrupt liberal gatherings. The former President Mahmoud Ahmedinejad, Ayatollah Mohammad Taqi Mesbah Yezdi (theoretician, mentor of Ahmedinejad, member 4th Assembly of Experts), Ayatollah Ahmed Jannati (Chairman of the Concil of Guardians, member of the Assembly of Experts), Ayatollah Mohammad Shahroodi (Chairman of the Judicial Branch, member of Assembly of Experts), Ayatollah Abolqasim Khazali (former member Council of Guardians, supported Ahmedinejad for president), Ahmed Pournejati, Massud Dehnamaki, Mehdi Nassiri, and Hossein Allah-karam supports the views of this group. The newspapers *Arzeshha, Kyhan, Lesrat al-Hossein, Shalamche,* and the monthly *Sobh* reflect their views.

However, Iran's polity has been broadly divided into two major blocs. While one bloc has been led by the Conservatives-Radicals Islamists coalition and other by the Moderates-Reformists Islamists coalition – each group contains both idealists and realists/pragmatics. The members of the *ulema's* positions in the post-revolutionary Iran are categorised after assessing their views on social, political, economic issues and their positions taken on these important issues.

From socio-economic perspective, Conservatives-Radicals Islamists and the Moderates-Reformists Islamists reflect the divergence of opinion within Iranian society. Both advocate for a strong political, economic and institutional presence within the public domain. The Conservatives-Radicals groups feel insecure in dealing with foreigners. The Moderates-Reformists groups are willing to compete, to influence, and be influenced. The confrontation between the two groups has produced a divided society, political deadlock and continued political radicalism.[6] The two groups have been continuously struggling in deciding the policy issues. This struggle has damaged Iran's image and projection beyond its borders.[7] Thus, political divisions have led to incoherency in policy formulation and its implementation.

Factions/Parties

From the beginning, the Islamic Republic has been a loose coalition of numerous factions, each representing specific and sometimes contradictory interests. The emergence of factions can be understood within the context of an Islamic pluralism, which has evolved within the history of the Islamic movement in Iran. This pluralism gave rise to political factions after the 1979 Revolution and particularly after the dissolution of the Islamic Republic Party (IRP) in June 1987. The constitutional revision in 1989 delineated the parameters of this pluralism. The backbone of some of the factions with close links to clergy and traders such as *Heyat-e Motalefeh-ye Islami* (HMI) (the Islamic Coalition Society, ICS) can be traced back to the early 1960s, while some others, like *Jame'eh-ye Ruhaniyat-e Mobarez* (JRM) (Association of Militant Clergy of Tehran, AMC), either emerged just before the Revolution in 1979 or, in the case of the *Sazman-e Mujaheddin-e Enqlab-e Eslami* (SMEE) (the Organisation of Endeavourer of Islamic Revolution, OEIR), immediately after. The HMI and the JRM seem like private members' clubs rather than political factions/parties. However, they have been very influential and comprise largely of traditional and far-right conservative clerics and lay-people with strong financial and social connections to the religious seminaries and *Bazzari*.

The Islamic Republic Party (IRP) was established in February 1979 and its offices were opened throughout country. It was an official political party in the Islamic Republic of Iran. Although the IRP emerged as a dominant political party after the first *Majlis* election in the Spring of 1980, and the country was heading towards one-party state. Iranian politics was effectively run by a number of influential figures within the IRP such as Ayatollah Mohammad Beheshti, Ayatollah Ali Khamenei (the current Supreme Leader) and Hashemi Rafsanjani.

The IRP did not continue for long and was dissolved. Ayatollah Khamenei and Hashemi Rafsanjani met Ayatollah Khomeini in June 1987, informed their intention to dissolve the IRP. They appraised Ayatollah Khomeini in that meeting about polarisation of the IRP and requested his assent to dissolve it. Ayatollah Khomeini was not happy with the activities of the IRP and realised the severity of the situation. As a result the IRP's activities came to an abrupt end due to internal divisions and polarisation.

The SMEE had good relation with Ayatollah Khomeini and the recruited members were initially founding members of the revolutionary guard. However, all political organisations loyal to the principles of the Islamic Republic and Khomeini's leadership, became part of one of the two major factions after the Revolution; the Followers of Emam's Line (FEL) which represented pretty bourgeois and was comprised of the SMEE, and a number of high ranking clergies like Ayatollah Musavi Ardebeli, Hojjatoleslam Musavi Khoeyniha, Mir Hussain Musavi and Hojjatoleslam Mohammad Khatami.[8] The second faction comprised of traditional religious conservatives, like the JRM and the HMI, which strongly connected with the Islamic Republic Part (IRP) and traditional *Bazzar*. The intra-elite factionalism began immediately after the Revolution that deepened and intensified.[9] The rivalry between all factions was contained by Khomeini and his presence stabilised the situation during the war with Iraq (1980-88) by shifting his political influence to the left (the FEL) and the right (the JRM and associates). Despite Ayatollah Khomein's efforts, intra-elite factionalism was intensifying, although slowly. The *Majma'-e Ruhaniyun-e Mobarez* (MRM) (the Assembly of Combatant Clerics, ACC) was the only major faction which emerged within the JRM in March 1988 to strengthen the FEL's position.[10] The factional politics continued during Khomeini, albeit limited.

Ayatollah Khomeini had preferred to remain aloof from conflicts of the elite and interfered only on rare occasions when the situation was out of control. Each faction sought to promote its policy preferences and clashed one another. Therefore, Khomeini started to issues decrees on social, political, and economic issues.[11] Most of the differences centred around domestic issues, especially economic issues. Islamic Republic of

Iran's foreign policy was a low priority among the factions in this period and clashes remained low. Foreign policy was injected into political clashes following the Iran-Iraq War ceasefire. The regime under leadership of Ayatollah Khomeini tried to present a united front but factionalism and conflict continued.[12] The cease-fire in the Iran-Iraq War in July 1988 added a new dimension to, and intensified, factional conflict.[13] Factional alignment began on reconstruction and foreign policy and intensified.[14] Factionalism in Iran further intensified after Ayatollah Khomeini's death on 3 June 1989.

With demise of Ayatollah Khomeini, political situation changed in Iran. In the absence of Ayatollah Khomeini, the ideological and political centrality of the system was weakened, and this paved way to the promotion of political factionalism.[15] In an interview, Hashemi Rafsanjani gave the reasons for the emergence of factions "may be a lot of people prefer to form factions instead of parties because in that case they do not need to be responsible to the people. In fact factions are taking the party's place. The members of these factions are saying something, and if they manage to gain a post, they think that they are not responsible for what they have said."[16] Hashemi Rafsanjani was known as a moderate member of the JRM until 1995.

The *Kargozaran-e Sazandegi* (KS) (the Servants of Reconstruction) was formed by the 16 ministers of the Rafsanjani Administration with his blessing. Rafsanjani's move was an expression of the disunity between the factions, which had reached a critical point. Such intense intra-elite factional politics continued to advance, and amalgamations of different factions formed a coalition before the May 1997 presidential election, known as the *Jebhe-ye Dovom-e Khordad* (JDK) (the Second Khordad Front, SKF). The newly formed organisation nominated a moderate clergy, Mahammad Khatami as their presidential candidate. Mohammad Khatami's policy polarised politics further. As a result, more that 100 new political organisations and parties/factions were born, among them the *Jebhe-ye Mosharekat-e Iran-e Islami* (JMII) (the Islamic Iran Participation Front, IIPF) formed and managed to get permission from the Article 10 Commission.[17] Numerous factions/parties were formed.

The sudden increase in the numbers of political organisations and Khatami's inability to implement reform provided fresh momentum to the rise of factionalism within the reformist and conservative camps. A major student organisation *Daftar-e Takhim-e Vahdat* (DTV) (the Office for Consolidation of Unity, OCU) broke its ties with the JDK in the summer 2003. Mehdi Karrubi formed his own party the *Hezb-e E'temad-e Milli* (HEM) (the National Confidence Party, NCP) in 2005.

With the 2003 local election, a new round of political polarisation emerged. The Far-Right elements (Radicals) within the traditional conservatives (members of the *Jamiyat-e E'sargaran Enqlab-e Islami*, with close ties to the Revolutionary Guard) started to gain electoral ground. Mahmoud Ahmedinejad was a high-rank man of this group who became mayor of Tehran in 2003. In 2004, during the seventh *Majlis* election the Far-Right elements (Radicals) formed the *Abadgaran-e Iran Islami* (AII) (Prosperity for Islamic Iran, PII). Relation between the *Abadgaran-e Iran-e Islami* and the new president, Mahmoud Ahmedinejad who was supposed to unite the conservative factions, became sour and during the 2006 local elections a new faction the *Rayehe-ye Khosh-e Khedmat* (RKK) (the Joyful Essence of Obedience, JEO) emerged in the support of the government within the Radicals Islamists. The rift between the AII and the RKK further widened during the eighth *Majlis* elections in 2008 and each became part of the different coalition.

Nature of Polity and Politics

Iran's political system came under religious influence since the religious community dominated the Revolution of 1979. Imamate system came into force with the creation of the position of the *Velaya-e Faqih*, and the clerics-rule established in the post-Revolution Iran. Ayatollah Khomeini became the *Velayat-e Faqih*. In 1979, the new regime under leadership of Ayatollah Khomeini pursued policies to accommodate various groups, organisations, and parties and their views in setting direction of domestic politics, but the Iran-Iraq War compelled Iranian leadership to negate dissents and their views. In Iranian leadership belief, dissentions during the Iran-Iraq War would pose serious threat to survival of the regime. Therefore, the regime banned those parties and organisations in 1981 whose activities were inimical to clerics-rule and integrity of Iran.

The regime established the Islamic Republic Party (IRP) in 1981, thus Iran headed towards a one-party system. When factionalism within the party intensified, Imam Khomeini ordered to dissolve the IRP in June 1987. However, the regime allowed various social organisations and factions to continue who were not considered threat to the regime. The political establishment in Iran, with all its factions, managed to dominate society since 1979, yet failed to draw up a sound policy to effectively resolve various social and political problems in the country. The Iran-Iraq War ceasefire, Khomeini's demise in June 1989 and new leadership at Tehran changed the domestic political situation. The concentration of power with Khomeini influenced the evolution of polity in the 1980s. With Khomeini's demise, power devolution began and polity changed. Power struggle among leaders started and intensified in the post-Khomeini period. The factions/groups started to present their views on political, social, economic, and cultural issues and each faction/group extended its support to one faction/group on one issue and favoured another on other issue at a time according to circumstances. Thus, the nature of Iranian polity is highly fluid since each faction/group changes its position as circumstances arise.

The fluid nature of Iranian politics appears/appeared in the policy statements of the Iranian leaders, as they have had different view on one issue and voice differently on another. The problem in Iranian polity, in fact is that particular individuals may take different positions on different issues and that has been seen since the Revolution. For instance, Ayatollah Sadeq Khalkhali, was internationally known as a hard-line extremist when it came to delivering justice to those who were considered enemies of the Revolution. On the other hand, Khalkhali was from the beginning strongly in favour of releasing the Americans held hostage at the US Embassy at Tehran between November 1979 and January 1981. While individuals were airing their different views on the issues, Imam Khomeini referred to the differences between the two groups as "two schools of thought", and Hashemi Rafsanjani called them "factions".[18] Individuals' different views on society, polity, economy, foreign policy, and security had been seen during the revolution which has been still witnessed. The same individual has different opinion on one issue and speaks in different voice on another issue. Many moderates shift their political positions to suit their immediate needs.[19] Individuals often change their positions over time, and it has been common for an influential religious leaders to speak one way and then to act in quite another way.[20] This type of opportunistic behaviour is a sign of an individual's personal interests which explicitly demonstrates fluid nature of Iranian politics.[21] Another example, former prime minister Mir-Hossein Mussavi was known as radical during the revolution, but now he is considered as moderate and contested the presidential elections in June 2009 against incumbent President Ahmedinejad, a hard-line conservative.

The leading clerics who best represented the political extremist category during Revolution were Ayatollah Ali Khamenei, Akbar Ali Hashemi Rafsanjani, and Ayatollah Mohammad Reza Mahdavi-Kani. Ayatollah Mohammad Reza Mahdavi-Kani was known as an extremist during the Revolution but these days he is considered as a traditional conservative. He was elected as the Chairman of the Assembly of Experts in March 2011 and held it till his death on 21 October 2014. Now Hashemi Rafsanjani is considered as moderate because of change in his thinking in the realm of foreign policy. In Iranian political culture, cautionary point is that the fluidity of Iranian politics is such that today's Conservatives-Radicals may be tomorrow's Moderates-Reformists and vice versa, and the Radicals on one set of issues may be Moderates on another. So, the nature of Iran's foreign policy is neither linear, nor dialectical, but *kaleidoscopic*.

One of the major features of Iranian polity is that political system provides space for factionalism and factional alliances. Factions and factionalism operate and thrive in Iran though their positions on different issues and their alliance with one another change depending on the circumstances or the nature of the issues at hand.[22] According to Daniel Brumberg, the Iranian political system functions as a dissonant system. He argues that "dissonant politics generates patterns of political change which do not move forward or backward along one clear line."[23] Brumberg refers to dissonant politics and argues that in these systems "divide and rule and elite accommodation are thus two sides of the same coin."[24] His arguments suggests that factionalism is an important ingredient for the stability of these systems since it can accommodate different factions and their interests within the system and at the same time those interest can compete one another. The accommodation of the various factions and their interests within the system reflects flexibility of the system and its survival tactics.

In Mehdi Mohsen's view, the politics of factionalism in Iran has been engaged in constantly reproducing itself since 1979.[25] The factional fighting reached a critical point during the eight years of Khatami's presidency. Political fighting during Khatami's presidency intensified and polarised politics within the elite beyond the point of no return. As political situation deteriorated, the conservatives withdrew their traditional power sharing policies. The continued political fighting among the factions demonstrates that the system in the Islamic Republic is unsettled. Hashemi Rafsanjani in a sermon at Tehran Friday prayers on 20 January 2000 said that the regime was in deep crisis due to power struggles among the factions. "When factions within the regime are at odds with each other, bring disrupt to one another, chanting slogans again one another, then wait and see who comes out on top. So, everyone is in a wait-and-see mood. This is not serving anyone's interests."[26] Rafsanjani explicitly sketched the feature of Iranian polity which continues to persist in Iran.

The role of political leaders in influencing each faction has been crucial for the Islamic Republic's internal affairs. Amongst the leaders, the roles of Ayatollah Khamenei and Hashemi Rafsanjani have been crucial in setting political priorities, forging political alignment and realignment, and for the policy making process in general. It is noteworthy that these two leaders founded the IRP and worked closely together for more than ten years (1979-92). Since then each has moved in different direction with varying followers. Rafsanjani, as a previous member of the JRM, distanced himself from the traditional conservatives, as the formation of the SOR indicated, and leaned towards reformists and the secularist forces.

One of the most powerful members of the ruling elite has been Hojatolislam Ali Akbar Hashemi Rafsanjani, who was the former Speaker of the *Majlis* (1981-89) and President (1989-97). Rafsanjani believes in *Rast-e Modern* but always oscillates between factions to serve his interests. Rafsanjani is the most versatile member of the ruling elites, easily switching back and forth between various factions depending on where his interest lies.[27] Being one of the ruling elites in Iran, he seeks to preserve his interests by supporting one faction against another. In order to maintain his influence, Rafsanjani wavered between the conservatives and moderates factions.[28] Iranian politicians change their views according to circumstances.

The fluid nature of Iranian politics is such that today's conservative may be tomorrow's moderate. The leading clerics who represented the political extremist category during Revolution were Ayatollah Ali Khamenei, Akbar Ali Hashemi Rafsanjani, and Mohammad Reza Mahdavi-Kani. Hashemi Rafsanjani changed over period of time, and now he is considered as moderate/pragmatists and he fought presidential elections June 2005 against Mahmoud Ahmedinejad after serving presidency twice (1989-1997). Hassan Rouhani, the current president of Iran, actually belongs to the Conservatives-Radicals Islamists groups, and now he has changed his views and joined the Moderates-Reformists Islamists groups. He received support during the presidential elections in June 2013 of the Moderates-Reformists Islamists groups. The former President Mohammad Khatami, ex-President Hashemi Rafsanjani, and moderates-reformists groups did not only extend their support in the June 2013 presidential elections to Hassan Rouhani, but also withdrew their presidential nominee. Indeed, he belonged to the conservatives section and the establishment, and was inducted in nuclear negotiations during the Khatami Administration from the conservatives side while it seemed that Khatami is going too far in nuclear negotiations with the West. Now Hassan Rouhani is considered as moderate and reformist within Iran and beyond.

The Iranian political system has been evolving into a bipolar system since the entire factions has divided into two blocs. The division into two blocs appeared in the early 1990s but the May 1997 presidential elections gave final shape. Factional politics further deepened and intensified during the Khatami period. By 2004, relations between the Conservatives-Radicals Islamist and the Moderates-Reformists Islamists further deteriorated and Iranian polity was polarised. The intense polarisation gave way to rise of the Conservatives, and finally the Conservatives-Radicals won the June

2005 presidential elections. In the June 2013 presidential elections, Hassan Rouhani got victory with the support of the Moderates-Reformists Islamists and Rafsanjani faction. It appears that domestic politics has been divided into two major blocs and each faction extends its support as it prefers. A bipolar system may solve some of the problems within the different factions for some time and may work up to a certain extent. Actually, Iranian polity carries broadly two blocs which run under the guidance and supervision of the Supreme Leader Ayatollah Khamenei.

Domestic Politics and its Dynamics

The Islamic Republic Party (IRP) was an official political party in the Islamic Republic of Iran though it emerged as a dominant political party after the first *Majlis* election in the Spring of 1980. Iran was heading towards one-party state. Iranian politics was effectively run by numerous influential figures within the IRP like Ayatollah Mohammad Beheshti, Ayatollah Ali Khamenei (the current Supreme Leader) and Hashemi Rafsanjani. The first *Majlis* was elected in the Spring of 1980 and which was first convened on 28 May of that year, 213 deputies were seated. Of 200 deputies, 43 were clerics. This number increased to 55 after the election of 24 July 1981, which was called to choose a new president and to find replacements for those deputies who had been assassinated in the bombing of 28 June 1981. This indicates that in the post-Shah, the *Majlis* had more cleric representation than any time in Iranian history.

In the first *Majlis*, the *ulema* held eight of the chairmanships and seven of the deputy chairmanships of the 23 parliamentary committees. The numbers of the *ulema* had been well represented in the major committees such as the Foreign Affairs Policy Committee, the Judicial Affairs Committee, the Defence Committee, and the Internal Affairs Committee. The powerful and very conservative Seyyid Ali Khamenei's brothers from Mashad represented on three of these critical committees. Sayyid Ali Hussein Khamenei chaired the Committee on Defence Matters and was a member of the Foreign Policy Committee, while Sayyid Muhammad Hassan Khamenei headed the Committee on Judicial Affairs. Both brothers were leading members of the Islamic Republican Party (IRP).

Besides *Majlis* representation, the *ulema* controlled important Cabinet portfolios. At the Cabinet level, Mohammad Reza Mahdavi-Kani and and Muhammad Javad Bahonar were in early 1981 Ministers of Interior and Education respectively. Before his assassination, Muhammad Javad Bahonar served for three and a half weeks as Prime Minister of the country and was in turn temporarily replaced in the post by Mohammad Reza Mahdavi-Kani in early September 1981. In Mahdavi-Kani's Cabinet, a cleric, Abol Majid Mo'adikhah, held the post of Minister of National Guidance. At the same time Seyyid Ali Hussein Khamenei became the new head of the IRP after both his predecessors (Muhammad Hussein Beheshti and Muhammad Javad Bahonar) were assassinated. In a very significant development, Seyyid Ali Hussein Khamenei was elected President of the Islamic Republic of Iran on 2 October 1981. As the internal political conflict deepened and the radical right entered into direct and violent conflict with the radical left, the members of the *ulema* became more and more deeply involved in political rule.[29] This kind of direct participation by the *ulema* in the formal national political arena, was the direct result of the dramatic events surrounding the continuing Iranian Revolution.[30] The presence of the clerics in the *Majlis* and ministries strengthened position of Ayatollah Khomeini in consolidating his power base.

Ayatollah Khomeini dominated Iranian politics till 1989 and he had run the country effectively. After Bani al-Sadr's departure, Sayyiad Ali Khamenei became the president, and run Iran with wishes of Ayatollah Khomeini. In the early 1979, Mehdi Bazargan became Prime Minister but the US embassy hostage crisis at Tehran on 4 November 1979 led his resignation on 6 November 1979. Prime Minister Rajai' could not lead Iran for long, and due to power struggle within Iranian politics had cost his job. Mir-Hussein Mussavi served the longest tenure of prime ministerial position but this post was abolished with the constitutional revision 1989 due to duality of power centres – President and Prime Minister – overlapping powers and functions between them.

In the 1980s, the country was effectively run by Ayatollah Khomeini since he led the masses in overthrowing the Shah. The Iran-Iraq War 1980-1988 and the foreign powers' role during the war sealed the fate of major dissention against Khomeini and his vision of state and government.

Opposition and dissenters were suppressed and marginalised in the 1980s. Iranian politics remained under firm control of Imam Khomeini and his associates. But some groups managed to survive with limiting their activities. With demise of Ayatollah Khomeini on 3 June 1989, the Islamic Republic entered into a new phase and a new leadership took charge at Tehran.

President Sayyiad Ali Khamenei became the Supreme Leader, and the *Majlis* Speaker Hashemi Rafsanjani elected as the president of the Islamic Republic in 1989. The new leadership tried to manage the Iranian economy since economy had severely suffered during the eight years war with Iraq. In order to improve economic conditions, Iran required mobilisation of domestic and foreign funds, technology, and assistance. Domestically, the issue of economic reforms and privatisation was intensely debated among the Iranians and the political groups/actions. Externally, capital and technology was available in the West and the US. Therefore, the new leadership offered rapprochement towards the West and the US to obtain foreign capitals and technologies. Both economic privatisation and relation with the US were fiercely debated within the political groups and entities, and political divisions deepened gradually. President Hashemi Rafsanjani tried to manage both the Conservatives-Radicals and Moderates groups, but leaned towards the Conservatives-Radicals in order manouvour political space since domestic politics was under control of the conservatives factions. Economic reconstructions led to entry of the domestic and foreign capitals. Consequently, it provided space for ideological divisions within Iran.

President Rafsanjani tried to weaken the Conservatives-Radicals in cooperation with some conservatives. He, in cooperation with some members of the Council of Guardians, orchestrated a move that led to the virtual disqualifications of several key Conservatives-Radicals Islamists from running candidates for the Assembly of Experts, which is responsible for the selection of the *Velayat-e Faqih*.[31] Several Conservatives-Radicals Islamists *Majlis* deputies, including Sadeq Khalkhali, who had pronounced death sentences in his capacity as a judge of the Revolutionary Courts in the early years of the Islamic Republic, and former Interior Minister Ali Akbar Mohtashemi were excluded from becoming members of the

Assembly of Experts.[32] Rafsanjani and his associates managed to weaken the influence of the Conservatives-Radicals Islamists again when the Council of Guardians disqualified a number of prominent Conservatives-Radicals from running as candidates for the Fourth *Majlis* elections scheduled for April 1992.[33] The list of approved candidates showed absence of some key Conservatives-Radicals Islamists *Majlis* deputies from the list, including several clerics such as Hadi Ghaffari and Sadeq Khalkhali.[34] Thus, Rafsanjani had weakened the Conservatives-Radicals Islamists in order to pursue his own policies without any hindrance. Nonetheless, several Conservatives-Radicals Islamists managed their candidatures. The three most noteworthy were the Majlis Speaker Mehdi Karrubi, Ali Akbar Mohtashemi, and Muhammad Musavi Koiniha.

Hojatolislam Ali Akbar Hashemi Rafsanjani Bahremani, the former Speaker of the *Majlis* (1981-89) and as the president (1989-1997), could not understand the repercussions of his policies that he initiated during his presidency. Rafsanjani's economic policies actually led to economic corruption and many private entities gained economic benefits from his initiatives. Political entities and politicians were aware about national economic misappropriation by certain private organisations and individuals. Particularly, economic issue moved the Islamic Republic in opposite direction that the conservatives groups could not understand. The last year tenure of President Rafsanjani witnessed a sharp division in society, and political polarisation and divisions actually translated into votes.

President Hashemi Rafsanjani began policies in the early 1990s that provided space for growth of political entities, and a number of organisations emerged by the mid 1990s. As economic and foreign capital investment issues began to debate, the growth of the political organisations intensified, and they gained firm ground by 1997. President Rafsanjani's policy failures, the rise of political organisations in the period and resentment of the masses against the government, led to the rise of the Moderates-Reformists in Iran. Moreover, deep political divisions among the political entities led to the rise of Moderates-Reformists in Iran's politics. The Moderates-Reformists political organisations and groups lent support to Mohammad Khatami in the May 1997 presidential elections. Mohammad

Khatami won presidential elections in May 1997 with landslide against the conservatives groups candidate Nateq-Nuri. Hashemi Rafsanjani's policies sharply divided the society that led to victory of the Moderates-Reformists groups in the presidential elections in May 1997. A new chapter opened in Iranian politics with victory of the Moderates-Reformists in the 1997 presidential elections.

Khatami's supporters comprised of several groups with diverse domestic and foreign policy agendas since he did not have an independent popular base of his own. The three main factions consisted of the modern Islamic left, the MRM a group of which Khatami himself was a founding member; the traditional Islamic left and remnants of the anti-Shah movement - *Mojahiddin-e Enqelab-e Islami* (Warriors of the Islamic Revolution); and the Modern-Right – *Kargozaran-e Sazandegi* (Workers of Reconstruction) – technocrats followers of ex-President Rafsanjani. The coalition of these diverse groups was formed since none were in a position in their own to stop Nateq-Nuri becoming the president. Once they succeeded in electing Khatami, each group expected him to protect and promote its interests and agendas. In Khatami's ministry, five out of 22 cabinet members and two out of seven vice-presidents were Rafsanjani loyalists, and former members of his team. In his ministry, four were from Mir-Musavi's wartime cabinet. Khatami also appointed Governor of the Central Bank who belonged to the Rafsanjani faction. He appointed Mir-Hussein Musavi, the wartime Prime Minister as his top adviser. As a result, while the Rafsanjani loyalists were bent on economic privatisation and marketisation, the other two Islamic left factions pushed for continued state intervention in the economy, large subsidies, foreign exchange controls and trade restrictions. There were often quarrels among the Ministry of Finance, the head of the Management and Plan Organisation, and the Governor of the Central Bank.[35] Thus, each group started to clash the other on policy issues and their implementations.

In Khatami's presidential election campaign, domestic agenda promised the dawn of an Islamic democracy where the theocratic concept of the *Velayat-e Faqih* would be reconciled with modern popular participation in decision-making. In the first two years of his presidency, political liberalisation and socio-cultural openness came to appear. In the domestic socio-political field, Khatami supported relative relaxation in the Islamic morals code (e.g., dress, music, social, social contact), increased openness in political discourse (e.g., newspapers, private news organisations, liberal periodicals, films, and use of the Internet), and greater attention to women's rights and their access to university education, employment, travel, and political participation.[36] The credit goes to Khatami for stressing on human dignity, establishment of political participation as both citizens' right and privilege, tolerance toward the loyal opposition, the growth of NGOs, holding nationwide municipal and village council elections, and democratisation of political power. The Khatami Administration's efforts to enforce Iran's constitutional guarantees of human rights and civil liberties were severely resisted and hampered by conservation-controlled institutions, partition judges, rough elements within the security forces, and vigilantes supported by radical clerics.[37] Thus, the 'rule of law' never effectively established.

The Khatami Administration encouraged the formation of political parties, allowed free labour unions, promoted secular professional associations, attempted to protect free press and political expression, and welcomed the rise of non-governmental organisations. On economic front, Khatami could not do well and suffered from contradictions, ambiguities, and lack of concrete plans. He reiterated the Khomeini line as basic principle that economic development should be tempered with social justice. He also stressed that growth should not be slowed down in the name of equity. His policy was a mixture of interventionist measures along with market-oriented proposals side by side.

Khatami allowed a space for political and social liberalisation, but he also failed to fulfil many of his promises. His reforms aimed at creating space to encourage people for participation in political process, thus their participation enhancement in the country's policy-making. Khatami's social and political liberalisation has had an irreversible impact on the post-revolutionary generation.[38] This in many ways was reflected in their participation in the June 2009 presidential elections, but more subtly in their preservance at creating a space for themselves despite the restrictions imposed during Ahmedinejad's presidency.[39] This was again demonstrated in the June 2013 presidential elections where they participated in large numbers.

Mohammad Khatami won the presidential elections twice with large mandates but could not fulfil the expectations of the people and his popular support base declined. However, Khatami and his Islamic left followers directed their efforts towards emphasising the sanctity of human rights, primacy of the rule of law, significance of political freedoms, importance of the free press, useful role of the NGOs, the propagation of the participatory Islamic democracy, and the need for dialogue of civilisations. Basically these issues were philosophically and ideologically important, but these appealed to a tiny intellectual and affluent minority, and especially privileged classes in the country. These issues had little or no relevance to the majority since they needed jobs, livable wages, affordable prices, low-cost housing, education, health care, and social security. Khatami's presidency transformed Iran's social, political and economic landscape without doubt but failed to address majority's aspirations and expectations.

Mohammad Khatami's detente policy and rapprochement with the world was severely resisted by the Conservatives-Radicals. His approach on domestic and foreign policies polarised and intensified Iran's polity and society.[40] It was the period when polarisation intensified on ideological basis. Particularly, in the Khatami presidency (1997-2005), the president's relatively open social and political policies had unintended consequences of heightening institutional and ideological competition among the country's political elites.[41] Iranian society after eight years of his tenure was more than ever polarised, alienated and cynical. It is true that Mahmoud Ahmedinejad won presidential elections not by guaranteeing freedom of speech and assembly but on his slogans of reducing poverty and economic disparity, employment, distribution of national wealth, health care, social justice, and social security.

One of the most powerful members of the ruling elite has been Ali Akbar Hashemi Rafsanjani, who is the ex-Speaker of the *Majlis* (1981-89) and President (1989-97). After that he served as the Chairman of the Expediency Council. Rafsanjani failed to win a seat in the 2000 *Majlis* election from Tehran despite a great deal of assistance from the Council of Guardians. He did not secure enough votes and came 32nd in the 30-seat Tehran district. The Council of Guardian disqualified on flimsy grounds the person with the highest number of votes and tried to disqualify numerous ballot boxes in order to raise and accommodate Rafsanjani, but ensuing media criticism forced Rafsanjani to withdraw his name. In the June 2005 presidential elections, Rafsanjani contested and lost to Mahmoud Ahmedinejad.

Mahmoud Ahmedinejad won presidential elections on promises of distribution of national wealth, reducing poverty and economic disparity, employment, health care, social justice, and social security. In presidential election campaigns his promises included justice, empathy service to people and improvements in the country's material and spiritual conditions. However, the main objectives included justice: fighting against poverty, corruption, discrimination and nepotism; progressing towards an Islamic society; and observing justice, peace and dignity in international relations.

Jahangir Amuzegar made observation on Mahmoud Ahmedinejad's victory in the June 2005 presidential elections in an article that "a self-made man from a large working-class family with brief civil service as a provincial governor and a controversial tenure as the mayor of Tehran, he won a stunning presidential victory in 2005 – trouncing four political giants, including a former two-time president and a pillar of the 1979 revolution."[42] It was really a stunning victory for a common man who defeated a heavy weight personality such as HojatolIslam Ali Akbar Hashemi Rafsanjani in the presidential elections 2005. Hashemi Rafsanjani was defeated in all provinces except Sisitan-Baluchistan province and even he was defeated in his home province Kirmanshah by Mahmoud Ahmedinejad in the June 2005 presidential elections.

Amuzegar further made his observation on victory of Ahmedinejad in the June 2005 presidential elections and characterised the nature of Iranian polity as "it was a normal swing of the ideological pendulum back to the right, reversing the leftward shift made in 1997 from Rafsanjani and a conservative *Majlis* to Khatami and his reformist coalition . . . it was a manifestation of the voters' disenchantment with Khatami's lacklustre and dissatisfying performance . . . who ignored the people's craving for both economic welfare and political participation."[43] The politics of factionalism entered into a new phase after the ninth presidential elections in 2005.

The presidential elections 2005 strengthened the Conservatives-Radicals Islamists and the Supreme Leader's position in particular.

Ahmedinejad as promised during election campaigns to introduce economic prosperity, social justice, distribution of national wealth among the poor and needy, eradication of economic inequality, creation of job opportunities, and health care. After assuming office, Ahmedinejad took several measures to improve economy and end corruption. He abolished the Planning and Budget Organisation, the purveyor of Iran's Five-Year Development Plans and preparation of fiscal budgets, and its duties were transferred to the president's office.

After assuming presidency, he tried to implement his promises which he had made during the presidential elections in June 2005, but faced severe resistance from the forces whose interests appeared to be undermined. He partially succeeded in implementing some promises made by him during the elections and funds allocated to *Buniyad Foundations* and widows and children of martyrs during the eight years of war with Iraq. He gave subsidy on several items such as gas, breads, foods, and transportation. He favoured toiling classes, labours, economically deprived, workers, and peasants. It seems, he followed the leader of the Revolution, Imam Khomeini, and made an attempt to eradicate corruption in the system and distribution of national wealth among the poor and needy. As Imam, Khomeini regularly emphasised the populism of Islam and constantly championed the rights of the downtrodden and lower-class masses. For instance, he gave an inspired speech on Workers Day 1 May 1979 "to my toiling brothers", "to all workers, men and women" in which he said, "our workers – the peasant class, the workers of the factories and those who work at other places – all activities going in the country, all things that are in this country, all the blessings of this country, all owe their existence to them; so they have precedence over all others."[44] Ahmedinejad argued the same and tried to distribute national wealth among the poor, needy, deprived, workers, and lower classes but was fiercely resisted by some forces.

Ahmedinejad's repeated slogans of 'justice, compassion, fairness and integrity' promising fair income and wealth distribution, increasing economic opportunities, and fighting corruption were welcomed by a large segment of the population. He called himself the people's 'servant' (*nokar*) and defender of the 'oppressed' (*mazloom*). He specifically promised to fight oil mafia and oil money on every body's table and reduce the size of government. He was a true supporter of the poor and underprivileged. In general, the conservatives believed that the Revolution had lost its way with the presidency of Rafsanjani and the pollution of revolutionary values through the introduction of rampant materialism and the corruption which accompanied it.[45] Ahmedinejad believed that the reform and reconstruction measures undertaken by Hashemi Rafsanjani and Mohammad Khatami had benefited some privileged segments of society and bypassed the masses. In his belief, oil money had been unjustly distributed. Some institutions got benefited from their policies.

The Islamic Revolutionary Guard Corps (IRGC) increased its presence in the administration and economy during Ahmedinejad tenure. Mahmoud Ahmedinejad gave place to the IRGC officers in his cabinet and awarded several economic projects to the IRGC during his presidency.[46] The IRGC became the largest economic enterprises in Iran in the tenure of Ahmedinejad. The IRGC is directly responsible to the Supreme Leader and looks after the Islamic Revolution which must be protected and preserved. It looks after and manages an entire security of the Supreme Leader, and its prime duty is to protect the position of the *Velayat-e Faqih*. Thus, Ahmedinejad protected and strengthened the position and status of Ayatollah Khamenei.

Iran's economy experienced a sea change during tenure of Ahmedinejad in the direction of economic militarisation. The Ahmedinejad Administration encouraged the Islamic Revolutionary Guard Corps (IRGC) for its participation in economic management and nation's economic building and allocated various contracts. The IRGC took over a number of economic projects and increased its presence in the Iranian economy. The *Khatamol-Anbia Corporation* and its sister, *Khatamol-Ossia*, the engineering arms of the IRGC, slowly became the largest and richest domestic contractors, and spreading their wings over sectors like oil, gas, petrochemicals, industry, mines, road construction, irrigation and dam construction. The UN, US, and EU sanctions targeted the IRGC, but their sanctions inadvertently helped the IRGC to grow by overtaking the work of foreign contractors, thus became the country's number-one economic holder. Economic privatisation was discouraged during Ahmedinejad presidency – only 17 percent of the state enterprises were sold to the true private sector, and 83 percent were taken over by the semi-public agencies.[47] The presence of the IRGC in the Iranian economy was even before, but its participation tremendously increased during Ahmedinejad presidency. The share of the IRGC in the economy increased ten-fold during his presidency.

Mahmoud Ahmedinejad dismissed several top officers during his presidency in order to eliminate corruption. He dismissed the technocrats assembled by his two predecessors and replaced them by officers from the IRGC and the *Basej*. The IRGC's rise has been accelerated since the 2005 election of President Ahmedinejad, himself a former IRGC commander. At one point of time, 12 of his 18-member cabinet were from these two organisations, and when his tenure ended six ministers were still former military and security officers. The IRGC's accumulation of political power is underpinned by growing economic and military influence. The IRGC has not only extended its influence into every sector of Iran's economy, including oil and gas sector, but also controls black market in economic sector.

The tenth presidential elections on 12 June 2009 intended to tighten grip and consolidate the Radicals' hold on power. Nonetheless, as the Conservatives-Radicals Islamists became increasingly involved in the control of power and policy, they subsequently became weaker internally. Their monopolist approach raised question over their legitimacy at home and abroad. The 2009 presidential elections exacerbated this situation as polarisation of politics caused mass protests. The result of the June 2009 presidential elections was contested and social and political divisions deepened. The event weakened not only the Conservatives-Radicals Islamists but also the Supreme Leader's position, where many clerics and politicians were concerned. Ayatollah Ali Montazeri and Ayatollah Asadollah Bayat issued a religious decree directly questioning the legitimacy of the Supreme Leader. Apparently, the factions' inability to manage some kind of safe level of political rivalry and the entry of the third force, the public, and their direct involvement in the political arena further exploited factional politics, and deepened the division between the two main factional blocs.

Ayatollah Khamenei is the Supreme Leader and pivot of the system. Ayatollah Khamenei's omnipresence in the system is not meant to be part of or in support of any particular faction, but he is directly involved time to time in factional politics and moved away from the traditional conservatives and their viewpoints, made alliances with the Conservatives-Radicals Islamists, which had close links with the Revolutionary Guard and ultimately in opposition to secular forces. Some political analysts argued against Ayatollah Khamenei's direct involvement in factional politics and support one against another. Political commentator like Abbas Milani has argued that Ayatollah Khamenei made a major error by ignoring his own supposedly unbiased position within the system and siding with Mahmoud Ahmedinejad in the tenth presidential elections June 2009.[48] Other political commentators like Majid Mohammadi observed that Ayatollah Khomeini had no choice but to declare his support to Mahmoud Ahmedinejad.[49] Actually Ayatollah Khamenei had no other option except landing his support to Ahmedinejad since result of the presidential elections 2009 had been declared and the two forces had been heading towards show of their strength. Ayatollah Khamenei intelligently took step to save the system.

Factionalism continued and further deepened though began immediately after election of Moahmoud Ahmedinejad as president in the June 2005. Rafsanjani remained an influential player in Iran's power politics and sought to succeed after Ayatollah Khamenei. Rafsanjani's bid for power set him up against Ayatollah Mohammad Taghi Mesbah-Yazdi, an archconservative and a mentor of Ahmedinejad. Mesbah-Yazdi was believed to want the Supreme Leader's job for himself and he lined up support among hard-line clerics for his own candidacy for the chairmanship of the Assembly of Experts in 2006. This dynamic produced a new alliance between the reformists and Rafsanjani.[50] Alignment and realignment continued and intensified after controversy over the June 2009 presidential elections.

As the rift between Ayatollah Khamenei and Rafsanjani deepened, politicians such as Mohammad Khatami, Mehdi Karrubi, and Mir Hussein Musavi who were initially associated with the FEL also shifted their views in favour of Moderates-Reformists Islamists, which became apparent after the June 2009 presidential elections crisis. These developments changed the political factions' positions and their supporters in two opposing poles. The June 2009 presidential elections crisis heated the political environment, displayed the insecurities and incompetence of factionalism within Iranian politics. Factionalism reached at its height and politics became so polarised that the factional differences simply could not be contained. The frustrations regarding the system and inability of factions to deliver coherent politics and what had been promised in 1979 'political freedom and social justice', spilled over onto the streets. A combination of different factors in conjunction of other developments fragmented the Iranian politics and pushed the fighting to the brink.

Factional divisions also appeared during Ahmedinejad presidency. Ahmedinejad helped in developing a split within the conservatives, separating the old-guard clerical elites had founded the revolution, formed a younger generation of veterans and laid Islamist idealists with uncompromising beliefs.[51] The power struggle among the Conservatives-Radicals Islamists reached at zenith after the tenth presidential elections 2009 when Ahmedinejad sacked reluctantly his first vice-president, Esfandiyar Rahim Mashia'. The removal of Esfandiyar Rahim Mashia' created fissures within the cabinet which angered Ahmedinejad leading him to sack four of his critics from ministerial posts, including intelligence minister, Hossayn Safar Harandi. Old-guard conservatives began to target Ahmedinejad's allies such as Deputy Foreign Minister Mohammad Sharif Malekzadeh, and the president's press advisor, the head of the Islamic Republic News Agency (IRNA) Ali Akbar Javanfekr.[52] In April 2011, Ahmedinejad demanded the resignation of the Minister of Intelligence, Heider Moslehi, but Ayatollah Khamenei stepped in and publicy rescined the resignation.[53] These developments put a question mark on Ahmedinejad's leadership and the government's credibility.

However, Mahmoud Ahmedinejad received praises of the Supreme Leader Ayatollah Khamenei who is pivot in the power structure of Iran.

The Supreme Leader Ayatollah Ali Khamenei had backed Ahmedinejad all along and found the ex-President's ideas close to his own. At the last meeting of Ahmedinejad cabinet with the Supreme Leader in mid-July 2013, Ayatollah Khamenei praised his government for its 'achievements in implementing people oriented policies and security issues', and for his propagation of 'revolutionary slogans'.[54] Ayatollah Khamenei extended support to Ahmedinejad since both subscribe the same views on crucial issues such as ideological, political, economic, social, and cultural.

Mahmoud Ahmedinejad has left his indelible imprint on Iran's politics and society by adopting a unique management style at home, and a defiant foreign policy towards the West.[55] Internally, he wrested power from the bureaucratic elites that had monopolised various levels of bureaucracy since the Revolution and gave it to his military and security men; shifted political forums from urban centres and sophisticated audience to small towns, deprived masses and less educated people; and took some independent political positions openly different from those of other government leaders. On economic front, the Ahmedinejad Administration discouraged privatisation of public undertakings. Serious and effective privatisation through the sale of state enterprises' shares to the public was resisted by almost all government agencies during the Ahmedinejad era. Iran's foreign policy had witnessed drastic changes, adopted confrontational policy, and built a new cadre of diplomatic envoys.

The continued power struggle among the factions divided the civil society. All factions have strong political and financial ties with influential members of the elite and have been engaged in advancing their interests through political alignment and realignment.[56] Each faction has its own publication linking their views to their followers.[57] Division within conservatives and people disenchantment against the Ahmedinejad Administration gave the rise to the Moderates-Reformists.

The factional struggle continued during the eight years of Ahmedinejad's presidency and reached to a critical point. After the June 2009 presidential elections, factions and groups started to organise and reorganise around the Moderates-Reformists bloc to defeat the Conservatives-Radicals bloc. The alliance among factions began to form in 2009 that evolved till 2012.

By 2013, the divisions among conservatives had appeared which replaced the Conservatives-Reformists split in the domestic political battle of Iran.[58] The conservatives section was divided. Hassan Rouhani contested the June 2013 presidential elections and got support of Hashemi Rafsanjani, Mohammad Khatami, and other moderates. The Moderates-Reformists did not only withdraw their candidate in favour of Hassan Rouhani in the June 2013 presidential elections, but also extended their support to him.[59] Divisions within conservatives and unity of the Moderates-Reformists helped Hassan Rouhani in the June presidential elections. Thus, Iranian polity can be understood as a fragile polity since the alliances form and re-form time to time depend on time and circumstances. The June 2013 presidential elections clearly reflects political dynamics in Iran and its impact over politics and political system

Conclusion

With changing Iran's political culture in 1979 its pattern of internal and external behaviour changed. Political process began following the Revolution that came under religious influence. Religion played a decisive role in shaping the post-Revolution Iran under leadership of Ayatollah Khomeini. Political trends emerged during the Revolution of 1979 which continued after that. The political trends - *Rast-e Sunnati, Rast-e Modern, Chap,* and *Rast-e Efrati* - influenced state behaviour. The forces debated on nature and character of polity, political system, social and economic issues, and security issues. With demise of Ayatollah Khomeini in June 1989, new leadership at Tehran tried to marginalise other political trends and factions, and succeeded, but could not marginalised for long, and emerged with reformist movement by 1997.

In the early 1990s, politics and the political system were completely dominated by the conservatives, but situation gradually changed. By the mid-1990s, circumstances changed and political polarisation on ideological line gained momentum. By 1997, political polarisation intensified and divisions took clear shape. The May 1997 presidential elections witnessed a sharp division between the two blocs – the Conservatives-Radicals Islamists and Moderates-Reformists Islamists. Iran experienced a bipolar polity for the first time with the May 1997 presidential elections. Political rifts could not remain with polity, but divisions also spilled over economic, social, foreign policy and security issues. Domestic political dynamics had influenced policy of the state during Hashemi Rafsanjani (1989-1997), Mohammad Khatami (1997-2005), Mahmoud Ahmedinejad (2005-2013). The result of the June 2013 presidential elections explicitly sketches domestic political dynamics and alignment and realignment of political forces and groups and its impact over the country's behaviour. Domestic political dynamics has been influencing state behaviour in the tenure of President Hassan Rouhani as before. The emergence of bipolar polity in the May 1997 presidential elections changed domestic politics and gave lasting impact over Iran's political system.

In political, economic, social, foreign policy, and security arenas, oscillation has been pattern, from one administration to the next and even within administrations as they experiment with diverse approaches. The pattern of interactions have witnessed changes from one administration to the next because of domestic political dynamics and changing factional equations. Policy differences appeared from one administration to the next. Political developments, domestic situation, and factions have been playing in shaping state behaviour, and will continue.

Endnotes

1   M Melkzadeh, *Tarikh-e Enqlab-e Mashrutiyat-e Iran*, Vols. 6 and 7 (Tehran: Elmi, 1373/1994), pp. 1328-9. Party views were published in Iran-e no for the democratic party and Enqlab for the conservative party.

2   Iran had several other party organizations in this period like Democratic Party of Azerbaijan (established in 1945 with close links to Tudeh party) and the National Will Party (headed by Seyed Ziauddin in 1943).

3   N R Keddie, *Modern Iran: Roots and Results of Revolution* (New Haven and London: Yale University Press, 2003), p.166

4   Ibid., p. 49

5   *Basiji:* Mobilisation Forces, a large volunteer force originally mobilized for the Iran-Iraq War 1980-88 and young students who are now organized to combat vice in society.

6   Mahmood Sarioghalam, "Transition In The Middle East: New Arab Realities And Iran", *Middle East Policy*, vol. 20, no.1, Spring 2013, pp. 124-127

7   Mahmmod Sarioghalam, "Iran's Emerging Regional Security Doctrine: Domestic Sources and the Role of International Constraints", in *The Gulf Challenges of the Future* (The Emirates Centre for Strategic Studies and Reaserch, 2005, pp. 163-184

8   The Followers of Imam's Line emerged after the revolution when the Islamic Republic Party (IRP) was established. Their members were closely identified with Ayatollah Khomeini's policies. This faction was different from other factions for its absolute obedience to Khomeini's leadership and his opposition to social and political freedoms under the pretext that they were manifestations of liberal democracy. When the IRP was dissolved by Khomeini, the ACC and the OEIR were amongst the factions claimed to be the Followers of Imam's Line.

9   Shahrough Akhavi, "Elite Factionalism In The Islamic Republic of Iran", *The Middle East Journal*, vol. 41, no. 2, Spring 1987, pp. 181-201

10 The ACC was founded on 20 March 1988, when some members of the Followers of Imam's Line among them Mehdi Karrubi, Mahmod Doai' and Ali Akbar Musavi Kho'eyniha, broke away from the CCA (see E'tema, 25 Azar 1386/2007 and Keyhan, 26 March 1988). The first secretary of the CCA was Ayatollah Mohammad Reza Mahdavi Kani and the ACC's first secretary was Mehdi Karrubi who resigned during the ninth presidential election in 2005 and formed the Hezb-e E'temad-e Melli (the National Confidence Party).

11 Maziar Behrooz, "Factionalism in Iran under Khomeini", *Middle Eastern Studies*, vol. 27, no. 4, October 1991, pp. 597-614

12 Akhavi, n. 9, p. 184.

13 Maziar Behrooz, "Factionalism in Iran under Khomeini", *Middle Eastern Studies*, vol. 27, no. 4, October 1991, p. 597

14 Ibid., p. 611

15 Kazem Almadari, "Hamiparvary Moshakhase-ye Ghodrat-e Siyasi", *Iran-e Farda*, vol. 44, 1377/1998, p. 10. Kazem Almadari views that death of Ayatollah Khomeini was the end of a populist system and the start of a clientelist system which was gradually replaced with a few leaders.

16 M Mohammadi, "Gozar as Mahfel be Hezb", *Iran-e Farda*, vol. 56, 1378/1999, pp-19-20

17 K Sardar Abadi, "Gozar be Towse'e Siyasi", *Aftab Magazine*, no. 2, Bahman1381/2002), p. 53. According to Mohammad Javad Haqshenas, an official in the Interior Ministry from may 1997 to March 2000, around 100

political parties got registration.

18   R K Ramazani, "Iran's Foreign Policy: Contending Orientations", *Middle East Journal,* vol. 43, no. 2, Spring 1989, p. 211.

19   Nader Entessar, "Factional Politics in Post-Khomeini Iran: Domestic and Foreign Policy Implications", *Journal of South Asian and Middle Eastern Studies,* vol. 17, no. 4, Summer 1994, pp. 22-23

20   James A Bill, "Power and Religion in Revolutionary Iran", *Middle East Journal,* vol. 36, no. 1, Winter 1982, pp. 35-36

21   Entessar, n. 19, pp. 21-23

22   Mehran Kamrava, "Iranian National-Security Debates:, Factionalism And Lost Opportunities", *Middle East Policy,* vol. 14, no. 2, Summer 2007, p. 84

23   D. Brumberg, "Dissonant Politics in Iran and Indonesia", *Political Science Quarterly,* vol. 116, no. 3, 2001, p. 408.

24   Ibid., p. 384.

25   Mehdi Mohsen, *Factional Politics in Post-Khomeini Iran* (New York: Syracuse University Press, 2002), pp. 3 and 47. He argues that in contrast to the revolution in Soviet Union and China (where factionalism was replaced by a strong central authority) factionalism had increased in Iran, each faction interprets its own version of Islam and Islamic government. In Mohsen's view, the rise of factions was primarily due to Khomeini's simple emphasis on the Islamic nature of the regime did not provide sufficient guidelines to determine the specific politics of the state, that is its socio-cultural policies, the nature of economic system and its foreign policy orientation.

26   ISNA, 22 January 2000.

27   Masoud Kazemzadeh, "Intra-Elite Factionalism and the 2004 Majles Elections in Iran", *Middle Eastern Studies,* vol. 44, no. 2, March 2008, p. 199

28   Saroghalam, n. 6, p. 125

29   James A Bill, "Power And Religion In Revolutionary Iran", *Middle East Journal,* vol. 36, no. 1, Winter 1982, p. 34.

30   Ibid.,

31   Entessar, n. 19, p. 29

32   Ibid.,

33   Ibid.,

34   Ibid.,

35 Jahangir Amuzegar, "Khatami's Legacy: Dashed Hopes", *Middle East Journal*, vol. 36, no. 1, Winter 2006, p. 73

36 "Iran Report", *Radio Free Europe/Radio Liberty*, 9 August 2005.

37 Amuzegar, n. 35, p. 66

38 Shabnam J Holliday, *Defining Iran: Politics of Resistance* (Farnham: Ashgate Publishing Ltd, 2011), p. 110.

39 Ibid.,

40 Amuzegar, n. 35, pp. 59-73

41 Mehran Kamrava, "Iranian National Security Debates: Factionalism And Lost Opportunities", *Middle East Policy*, vol. 14, no. 2, Summer 2007, p. 88.

42 Jahangir Amuzegar, "Ahmedinejad's Legacy", *Middle East Policy*, vol. 20, no. 4, Winter 2013, p. 124

43 Jahangir Amuzegar, "The Ahmedinejad Era: Preparing For The Apocalypse", *Journal of International Affairs*, vol. 60, no. 2, Spring/Summer 2007, p. 35

44 For the text of Imam Khomeini's Worker's Day speech, see *The Message of Peace*, 13 Rajab 1399/8 June 1979, pp. 16-18

45 Ali M. Ansari, "Iran Under Ahmedinejad: The Politics of Confrontation", *Adelphi Paper 393* (London: IISS, Routledge, 2007), p. 69

46 Amuzegar, n. 42, pp. 124-132

47 www.jamhourieslami.com, 7 November 2013

48 *Voice of America (VOA) TV*, 17 August 2009.

49 *Voice of America (VOA) TV*, 17 August 2009.

50 Bahman Baktiari, "Iran's Conservative Revival", *Current History*, vol. 106, no. 696, January 2007, pp. 12-13

51 Clifton W. Sherrill, "Why Hassan Rouhani Won Iran's 2013 Presidential Election", *Middle East Policy*, vol. 21, no. 2, Summer 2014, p. 67

52 Ibid., p. 69

53 Ibid.,

54 www.radiofarda.com, 1 August 2013.

55 Amuzegar, n. 43, p. 35

56 Part of their financial support comes from the government. Ahmedinejad put an end to this practice since 2005, but shifted his weight towards the

pro-government organizations. Prior to the tenth presidential election, he was accuse of spending cash from the budget to garner support for his own faction.

57 The ICS, Resalat; the NCP, E'temad-e Milli; the CCA, Aftab-e Yazd; the SOR, Kargozaran; the OEIR, Asr-e No and the IIPF, Moshareqat used to publish respectively. All factions also closely associate with various religious seminaries and Grand Ayatollah's for spiritual support and religious legitimacy. For instance, almost all pro-reform factions are close to Ayatollah Ali Montazeri, moderate conservatives are linked to Hashemi Rafsanjani and other Grand Ayatollahs like Abdolkarim Musavi Tabrizi and Yousef Sanei' while the Pricipalists' support comes from Mohammad Taqi Mesbah Yazdi and Mohammad Yazdi.

58 Clifton Sherrill, "Why Hassan Rouhani Won Iran's 2013 Presidential Election", *Middle East Policy*, vol. 21, no. 2, Summer 2014, p. 70

59 Ibid., pp. 64-75

Chapter - 3

Domestic Politics Impact over Foreign Policy

There are two dominant analytical tendencies that have impeded a fuller comprehension of the Islamic Republic's foreign policy. These two tendencies are thoroughly debated within academia and policy-makers to understand a comprehensive foreign policy of Iran. One views foreign policy of the Islamic Republic as a mirror image of its 'domestic politics.' The other sees Iran's foreign policy mainly in terms of 'geopolitics.' An examination of Islamic Republic of Iran's words and deeds and its theories and practices makes clear that Iran's foreign policy has been shaped largely by interplay of domestic situation including factional politics and external environment.

There are four main political trends – *Rast-e Sunnati* (the Traditional Right), *Rast-e Modern* (the Modern Right), *Chap* (the Left), and *Rast-e Efrati* (the Radical Right) – under which each faction operates, and makes an endeavour to influence the foreign policy. Each faction has its own approach and agendas in relation to the country's foreign policy. However, the discourse on Iran's foreign policy has been broadly divided into two major streams while one stream has been led by the Conservatives-Radicals Islamists and other by the Moderates-Reformists Islamists. Iran's foreign policy has been an arena of consistent factional debates and disagreements. They include Iran's relations with the US and the West, the US goals and agendas in the West Asia in general and Iran in particular, Iran's relations with Israel, Iran's regional standing, its regional policy, relations with Iraq, ties with Syria, relations with *Hizb-e Allah*, and Iranian-Hamas relations. Domestic political dynamics continue to sway foreign policy of Iran despite consistency in the regime and stable political system.

At the outset, Ayatollah Khomeini, the leader of the Revolution 1979, set direction and agendas of Iran's foreign policy. With demise of Imam Khomeini in June 1989, Ali Khamenei became the Supreme Leader. Ayatollah Khamenei's personal background, experiences, and developments, has shaped his foreign policy orientation.[1] After the Revolution, Ali Khamenei survived an assassination attempt which permanently disabled his right hand.[2] Ayatollah Khamenei's experiences have shaped Iran's foreign policy as Ayatollah Khomeini. However, other factors also continue to influence foreign policy of the Islamic Republic.

No doubt, there are also other factors which directly and indirectly influence country's foreign policy. There are variable and invariable factors like Iran's size, geo-location, geo-politics, economic resources, economic development, science and technology, geo-political developments, regional developments, international developments, and international system. They have been consistently impinging on foreign policy of the Islamic Republic irrespective of factional approaches in relation to Iran's external relations. However, factional debates over Iran's foreign policy have been consistent since the Revolution 1979 and each faction has been struggling to influence it. Even in the Khomeini period, the debates over foreign policy had been continuing. Ayatollah Khomeini provided space for debates over foreign policy, but he was final arbitrator in relation to Iran's external relations. Now Ayatollah Khamenei has been playing the same role as Ayatollah Khomeini did.

The early period of the 1979 Revolution did not decide only domestic politics but also foreign policy of Iran. The streets had played decisive role in determining foreign policy of Iran. The Conservatives-Radicals Islamists had held control over the Iranian streets, thus decided direction, orientation, and objectives of Iranian foreign policy. The new regime gave slogan of 'Neither West Nor East' in maintaining its external relations and 'complete independence' in pursuit of foreign policy. However, the regime later soften its stance in maintaining relations toward the East, but remained in opposition to Iran's relations with the West. The moderates had been consistently arguing in favour of Iran's relations with the West and raising their voices regarding foreign policy, but they could little do. The attitudes of the United States and the West towards Iran and the Iran-Iraq War provided opportunity to the Conservatives-Radicals Islamists to prevail over the Moderates-Reformists Islamists. As domestic politics slowly changed, the debates on Iran's foreign policy gradually intensified, and the voices of the Moderates-Reformists Islamists were considered.

The post-Revolution foreign policy of Iran has been based on a number of cherished ideals and objectives embedded in the constitution of the country. These comprise preservation of Iran's independence, territorial integrity, national security, and sustainable national development. Externally, the Islamic Republic seeks to enhance its regional and global stature; to promote its ideals and Islamic democracy; to expand its bilateral and multilateral relations, especially with Muslim-majority countries and nonaligned states; and to promote peace and security at regional and international levels through positive engagement. The victory of the 1979 Revolution produced a new kind of political culture and order in the country. The repercussions were drastic, and the Revolution deeply affected Iran's foreign relations not only with neighbouring countries, but also the entire West Asia and the world.

With demise of Ayatollah Khomeini in June 1989, President Ayatollah Khamenei became the Supreme Leader of Iran, and Hashemi Rafsanjani elected as president of the Islamic Republic. Mohammad Khatami succeeded Hashemi Rafsanjani as president of Iran in1997. Mahmoud Ahmedinejad elected as president of Iran in June 2005 and June 2009 presidential elections and remained till July 2013. Hassan Rouhani was elected as president in the June 2013 presidential elections and is still serving. Iran's foreign policy witnessed a platonic shift as a new administration installed at Tehran. The shifts in the Islamic Republic's foreign policy clearly reflect the effects of domestic political dynamics on Iran's external behaviour. Each president carried supports of its respective factions and did not receive supports of all factions. Thus, each president made and executed its external policy as the faction he belonged. Therefore, Iran's foreign policy has witnessed the effects of domestic political dynamics in all these periods while remaining the Supreme Leader Ayatollah Khamenei as a final arbitrator.

Iran's foreign policy has been vertically divided into two streams and each seeks to pursue its own agenda in maintaining relations with the foreign countries. This has been a peculiar feature of Iran's foreign policy since 1979 which still continues. All factions profess an Islamic identity and display commitments to the principles of the constitution of the Islamic Republic. They have unanimous views over survival of the Islamic Regime, but they pursue different foreign policy approach. Each has its own approach and agenda in relation to the country's foreign policy. The struggle between the Conservatives-Radicals Islamists and the Moderates-Reformists Islamists has been still continuing in determining Iran's foreign policy issues, as had been in the past.

Divisions in Setting Direction of Foreign Policy

When Mohammad Reza Shah left Iran, the new leadership in Tehran sought to set direction of the country's domestic and foreign policy. Divisions among the new ruling class emerged and became gradually deep and sharp in relation to setting direction of domestic politics and foreign policy. Imam Khomeini, leader of the Revolution, dominated policy formulation arena and devised foreign policy orientations. The dominant position of Imam Khomeini restricted other forces to free play in matter of policy formulation. Imam Khomeini managed divisions among the new ruling elites in setting direction of foreign policy. But divisions among the new ruling elites in relation to foreign policy remained and continued even after death of Imam Khomeini. This division among the ruling elites is still continuing and is likely to continue in the future.

When Imam Khomeini appointed Mehdi Bazargan as the provisional prime minister on 5 February 1979, the first priority of his government was to terminate the subservient de facto alliance of the Shah's regime with the United States and place the relations of the two countries on an 'equality' basis. He crafted his foreign policy on the basis of 'tavazon' (equilibrium), a principle dating back to 1848-1851 when it was first introduced into Iranian foreign policy thinking and practice by Mirza Taqi Khan, known as Amir Kabir, during his short-lived premiership in Nassirudin Shah Qajar period.[3] Mehdi Bazargan pursued a nonalignment policy. In his belief, Iran's policy towards the Great Powers should be the same as the policy of Mohammad Mussadeq. Mohammad Mussadeq adopted policy of 'muvazeneh-e manfi' (negative equilibrium). Mussadeq's nonalignment policy intended at maintaining Iran's independence by teminating British domination. Mehdi Bazargan sought similarly to end Washington's dominant influence by undoing the Shah's de facto alliance with the United States. According to new regime's first foreign minister, Karim Sanjabi, Iran's nonalignment policy was based on four pillars: "history, the country's geographical position, the spiritual and humanist ideals of Islam, and the principle of complete reciprocity in relations with other countries."[4] Thus, the new regime sought to maintain an independent foreign policy.

Karim Sajabi's National Front and Mehdi Bazargan's Iran Liberation Front both were nationalist, secular, and democratic in nature, drawing their social support largely from the middle classes and the modern-educated intellectuals. For both of them, the basis of people's loyalty to polity was considered to be the Iranian nation-state. Bazargan viewed that he could be called an 'Iran first' while Imam Khomeini was an 'Islam first'. In Bazargan's words, "I believe in the service of Iran by means of Islam" while Imam Khomeini "believes in the service of Islam by means of Iran".[5] The clear differences between the two leaders, which existed, surfaced openly at the outbreak of the hostage crisis. Mehdi Bazargan resigned immediately after seizure of US Embassy at Tehran on 4 November 1979.

Despite deep resentment of the Carter Administration's continuing support to the Shah, Bazargan tried to pursue a nonalignment and non-hostile policy towards the United States. To end the Shah's de facto alliance with the US, Foreign Minister Karim Sanjabi withdrew Iran's membership from the Central Treaty Organisation (CENTO) on 12 March 1979. Sanjabi was replaced by Ibrahim Yazdi as foreign minister. Foreign Minister Ibrahim Yazdi on 3 November 1979 cancelled the Iran-US Defence Agreement of 5 March 1959. To end the Shah's de facto alliance was substantively required to end a complex web of military relationships with the US built up over the years by the Shah. On the same day that the Bazargan government cancelled Iran's defence agreement with the US, it also abrogated Articles V and VI of Iran's 1921 treaty with the Soviet Union. After 6 November 1979 resignation of Bazargan, this cancellation was affirmed on 10 November 1979 by the Revolutionary Council.

Mehdi Bazargan resigned on 6 November 1979 but his policy of nonalignment did not disappear with his resignation. Iran's foreign policy split down the middle between the two major orientations. Both Abol

Hasan Bani al-Sadr, first as acting foreign minister and then as the first president of Iran, and Sadeq Qotbzadeh, Iran's foreign minister, took a foreign policy line that was close to the nationalist nonalignment policy of Mussadeq and Bazargan. Although Abol Hasan Bani al-Sadr rationalised his 'equidistance' policy in Islamic terms, he would rely on Western Europe or France as a counterbalance to the superpowers.[6] Bani al-Sadr believed that "despite the historical and ideological differences between the West and Iran, the two sides interests were not so far apart."[7] In Bani al-Sard's view, differences exist, but both sides continue their business with each other. Abol Hasan Bani al-Sadr had been continuing policy as had pursued by Mehdi Bazargan. All Iranian leaders, in the realm of foreign policy, were hostage of domestic popular sentiment.

Iran's Foreign Minister Sadeq Qotbzadeh, no less than his archrival Bani al-Sadr, believed in a nonalignment policy, using the Mussadeq term *'movazneh manfi'* (negative equilibrium) with what he called "honesty in word and in deeds."[8] Besides 'negative equilibrium', Sadeq Qotbzadeh listed the other principles of Iran's foreign policy as follows: "non-interference in affairs of other countries; a policy of an independent Iran; independence in decision-making; and harmonizing ideology and politics."[9] They, like their predecessors – Mussadeq, Bazargan, Sanjabi, and Yazdi, who preferred the word 'positive neutralism' – were all nationalists. As such they were all opposed by the Conservatives-Radicals Islamists who claimed to follow *'khat-e Imam'* (the Imam Khomeini line). Such as, Iran's foreign policy was determined by domestic situation rather than coherent policy formulation.

Indeed the Conservatives-Radicals Islamists were the architect of foreign policy orientations. They used *Khat-e Imam* in setting direction of domestic politics and foreign policy. The Conservatives-Radicals Islamists interpreted Imam Khomeini's policy statements to suit their own interests. Thus, divisions among the revolutionaries remained and persisted in setting foreign policy orientations. For instance, at the time of US Embassy hostage crisis at Tehran in November 1979, the divisions among the new ruling elites appeared in relation to foreign policy. This division further deepened and intensified. Iranian society and the ruling elites have divided pertaining to foreign policy issues, particularly relations with the US, and the divisions have been still continuing on these issues. The Conservatives-

Radicals Islamists are closely watching each move of President Rouhani in relation to Tehran-Washington relationship. Thus, divisions among the ruling elites in relation to foreign policy appeared in the early 1980s that have been persisting even during the Rouhani period.

Iranian Streets and Foreign Policy

The revolutionaries and streets had decided direction of Iran's foreign policy in the early 1980s. Undoubtedly, Iran's external policy was determined by sheer domestic compulsion. The dominance of the streets illustrated the 444-day hostage crisis, and was a clear confrontational path. The seizure of the US Embassy in Tehran on 4 November 1979 was a clear reflection of deep resentment against the United States. The seizure of the US hostages on 4 November 1979 not only antagonised the US, but also transformed the very nature and character of Iran's foreign policy. In the words of its first prime minister, Mehdi Bazargan, the Khomeini regime's stance changed from "defensive" to "confrontational".[10] The new regime's foreign policy was guided by sentiment and overturning everything. In the early days of the Revolution, the revolutionaries were confrontational in their approach because of deep resentment against the Shah's regime and the US/West. Before the seizure of the US Embassy, Bazargan had made efforts to build Iran's new relationship with the US on the basis of the principle of 'equality'. After downfall of his government on 6 November 1979, Tehran's relationship with Washington further suffered and hostility increased. Bazargan's nonalignment policy was nationalistic and accommodating, based on the historic principle of equilibrium. As such, Bazargan sought to maintain Iran's independence within the context of the existing international order. The new regime's orientation in essence defied that system, conventions and norms of diplomatic behaviour, and its international law. The 'student-captors' of the US hostage were the original architects of this 'confrontational foreign policy', an orientation continues to date within the ruling political elite and certain non-elite factions of Iranian political culture.

The takeover of US Embassy reflected in part the division between the Radical Islamists factions and the Moderates Islamists. The Radical Islamists attacked Bazargan's policy of nonalignment, accusing him and his foreign minister of pro-US. The revolutionaries seized power from the Shah on 9 February 1979, and only three days after the seizure of power by the revolutionary forces, the US Embassy was attacked for the first time. After a couple of days, US Ambassador William Sullivan and some other Americans were freed as a result of Iranian foreign minister Ibrahim Yazdi and others in Khomeini's entourage. President Carter's admission of the Shah to the US on 22 October 1979 triggered a massive anti-American demonstration in Iran and whose goal of attacking US Embassy was averted. But on 4 November 1979, the anti-Bazargan forces used the excuse of a meeting held in Algiers between Mehdi Bazargan and Ibrahim Yazdi with the then US National Security Advisor Zbigniew Brzezinski as a pretext to attack and occupy the embassy of the United States. Imam Khomeini endorsed the seizure of the US Embassy. Imam Khomeini's approval of the embassy seizure was an ample reflection of the confrontational path of regime's foreign policy. Imam Khomeini's endorsement of the embassy seizure raised both domestic and external concerns. At the time, their action was emotionally popular and had mass support base.

President Bani al-Sadr worked hard to transfer control of the hostages from their captors to the government so as to obtain their eventual release. He and Sadeq Qotbzadeh were working hard for the release of the hostages from the captors. At Bani al-Sadr's urging, the Revolutionary Council recommended (by a vote of eight to three) the transfer of the hostages to government control, only to be rejected by Imam Khomeini. He was supporting the students for the same reasons that he endorsed the seizure of the US Embassy in Tehran.

Meanwhile the Iranian leadership realised that the prolongation of the hostage crisis would not further serve Iran's interest. The West Germany had maintained good relations with new regime proved a valuable asset in settling the hostage dispute. Sadeq Tabatabai made contact with the German Ambassador in Tehran, whom he knew well, and sought his mediation to meet with US representatives regarding this. This contact was arranged through Bonn and proved to be the first move in the process of negotiations that finally led to the release of the US Embassy hostages.[11] However, Hashemi Rafsanjani was the most influential leader after Imam Khomeini, and he played the central role in the 1981 hostage settlement between Iran and the US. The settlement of the hostage crisis (4 November 1979 - 21 January 1981) ended the students' control of Iran's US policy, a control that could not have been sustained for long without blessing of Imam Khomeini.

The streets had been continuously playing an important role in setting direction of the country's foreign policy since 1979. The leadership used streets throughout the 1980s to garner support on a particular issue and policy, and this strategy was continued in the 1990s and after. The ex-President Hashemi Rafsanjani's supporters formed organisation named *Kargozaran-e Sazandegi* to mobilise mass support on issues that played largely at the streets in the form of protests and demonstrations. The moderate forces also came at streets and organised protests and demonstrations to show their policy preferences in the 1990s and 2000s. The former president Mohammad Khatami supported the moderate forces directly and indirectly in organising street protests and demonstrations.

The ex-President Ahmedinejad's statements against the US, the West, and Israel did not receive streets supports not only within Iran, but also from the Arab streets and others. His statements against Israel and anti-US stance received praises within Iran and many parts of the world. Apparently, the streets have been playing a vital role in setting direction of the Islamic Republic's foreign policy since 1979. Undoubtedly, the relevance of Iranian streets has not yet eroded, and has been still playing a vital role in determining the country's foreign policy as the 1980s.

Confrontational Foreign Policy

The outbreak of the Iranian Revolution 1978 reflected as much nationwide opposition to the Shah's foreign policy as to his domestic politics. The attack of opposition on his foreign policy centred on his de facto alliance with the United States and hence the revolutionaries referred to him, as 'the American King'. Although the roots of the 1978-79 Revolution are myriad and traceable, is beyond the scope of study in this paper. Indeed, the confrontational foreign policy's seeds were sown in the pre-Revolution period, but actually ushered during the Revolution and after.

The Iranian leadership worried on the US and the West attitudes towards Iran. The new regime in Iran was concerned with the Carter Administration's anti-revolutionary stance. Imam Khomeini was suspicious of every move Washington made in the realm of Gulf security and stability. These moves included Secretary of Defence Harold Brown's visit to the West Asia (9-19 February 1979) which took place at the time of the revolutionary regime's seizure of power and his statement that the United States would itself defend its vital interests in the region by military force. They also included the US negotiations with Somalia, Kenya, and Oman for military facilities, and the dispatch of the USS Constellation and several supporting warships to the Indian Ocean and Arabian Sea, as well as strengthening of the small US naval force in the Gulf itself. Another interpretation of the Carter Administration's military force deployment and movement in the region was to check the Soviet Union's westward expansion since the Soviet Union had intervened militarily in Afghanistan in December 1979 and brought that country under its control.

The US move in the region and around was noticed by Iran's new regime, and leadership in Tehran worried at the US policy statements. In fact, Imam Khomeini and entourage were concerned with the US and the West since the US and the West were averse to the Islamic government in Iran. The *ulema* dominated the Revolution since the Shah did not leave space for activities of any organisation except religious organisations. Thus, religious community penetrated into system and set direction, orientation, and priority of the country's domestic politics and foreign policy. The Conservatives-Radicals Islamists used all avenues to influence and determine foreign policy agenda as domestic politics.

The Conservatives-Radicals Islamists were the architects of the major foreign policy orientation. They interpreted Imam Khomeini's policy statement to suit their own interests. Their interpretation of Imam Khomeini's policy statements involved, above all else, two major foreign policy issues – Iran's relations with the West and the East and Iran's export of the 'Islamic Revolution'. Imam Khomeini stated on 9 December 1979, "A nation that cries in unison that it wants the Islamic Republic, it wants neither East nor West but only an Islamic Republic . . . we have no right to say that the nation that engaged in an uprising did so in order to have democracy . . . ."[12] He issued this statement at the height of the Azerbaijani crisis over the adoption of new constitution. Imam Khomeini had put emphasis that Iran should not blindly imitate Eastern socialist or Western capitalist modles, and claimed that 'Islamic democracy' is superior to both Eastern and Western democracies. The Conservatives-Radicals Islamists interpreted the issue differently and used the term 'neither East nor West' to advocate that Iran should not maintain relations either with the Soviet Union or the United States, nor with the governments closely associated with the superpowers.

The new regime pursued 'neither East nor West' policy which centred at maintaining independence from both. However, Iran's confrontational foreign policy did not end with the settlement of the US hostage crisis in January 1981. Iran suspected the US move in the region as destruction of the Islamic regime. In Iran's belief, increasing activities of the US in the Persian Gulf beginning as early as February 1979, aimed to contain and destruct the new regime. The Iranian saw the US as a real instigator of the Iraqi invasion of Iran on 22 September 1980. In their view, the war was 'imposed' by the US 'deputy', Saddam Hussein. In the entire period of the Iran-Iraq War, the Conservatives-Radicals Islamists' foreign policy orientations prevailed over that of the Moderates Islamists.

By June 1981, Imam Khomeini and his followers institutionally and relatively consolidated their power. The first *Majlis* was elected in the Spring of 1980, and first convened on the 28 May that year. Institutionally, power had been relatively consolidated – with the adoption of the constitution, the election of the first president, the election of the first *Majlis* and its first speaker by September 1980. The ideological and political struggle between Bani al-Sadr and his supporters and the triumvirate of Mohammad Beheshti, Mohammad Ali Raja'i, and Hashemi Rafsanjani and their followers became more acute after the settlement of the hostages crisis. President Abol Hasan Bani al-Sadr was forced to flee to Paris in 1981 and Sadeq Qutbzadeh (foreign minister) was also executed in 1981.

The two factions continued to operate, and struggled to determine policy issues. Initially, these two factions were more visible on domestic economic issues than on issues of foreign policy and military. But gradually these two factions sharply divided on the issues of military and foreign policy. However, it was no secret that the questions about the division of labour between the regular military and the Islamic Revolutionary Guard Corps (IRGC, popularly known as the *Pasdaran*) sparked fierce debates from the beginning of the war.

Iran's confrontational foreign policy continued and the "export of the revolution" and annual demonstrations during the *Haj* in Saudi Arabia isolated Iran within the region, as did its dispatch of Revolutionary Guards to Lebanon and its support of the Lebanese *Hizb-e Allah* and *Islamic Amal*. Moreover, the holding of American, British, French, and German hostages in Lebanon by the reputed pro-Iranian groups, and their confrontational policy, further isolated Iran. The new regime pursued confrontational policy since the Revolution of 1979 centred at the opposition to the Shah's domestic policy and his relations with the US and the West.

Students pursuing the export of the revolution, in defying the wishes of Foreign Minister Qotbzadeh, sponsored an international conference of 16 national liberation movements from across the world. Like other revolutionary idealists, Mohammed Montazeri, the late son of Ayatollah Hossein Ali Montazeri, organised the Iranian Revolutionary Organisation of the Masses of the Islamic Republic and sought to dispatch Islamic fighters to Lebanon as early as December 1979, long before the Revolutionary Guards were sent there in 1982. He was opposed by President Bani al-Sadr and Foreign Minister Sadeq Qotbzadeh just as was done by Mehdi Bazargan.

The idiom of the export of the revolution, furthermore, aggravated problems in Iran's relations with the Soviet Union. The ethnic and geographical proximity of the two countries raised the Soviet Union's concern about the effects of the Islamic Revolution among Soviet Muslims. In reality, both the United States and the Soviet Union sought to contain Iran's Islamic Revolution. The US allies in the region and beyond perceived threat from the Islamic Revolution in Iran whereas the Soviet Union feared instability in its Muslims inhabited provinces.

The new regime did not care about Iran's international isolation due to its confrontational foreign policy. The State's behaviour was completely dictated by the domestic compulsions and the forces seized the power from the Shah. These idealists repeatedly referred to one of Imam Khomeini's statements to buttress their foreign policy orientation: "We must become isolated in order to become independent."[13] The *Majlis* Speaker, Hashemi Rafsanjani lodged complaint that such statements are often quoted out of context. Imam Khomeini made this statement at the time of the US Embassy hostage crisis at Tehran when, in fact, Iran had become internationally isolated partly because of the Western diplomatic sanctions and partly because of the disapprobation voiced by the UN Security Council and the International Court of Justice.

Just as Iran has had its revolutionary idealists since the beginning of the Revolution, it has had revolutionary pragmatists too. Both believe that Islam is, and should be, the prime unit of people's loyalty in the Iranian polity, but they sharply differ/differed on the relative weight of the 'Iranianness' and 'Islamicness' in the Iranian identity. They differ/differed towards the international system as domestic politics. The Conservatives-Radicals Islamists prefer Islam over other things. On the other hand, the Moderates Islamists, knowing the existing realities, sought to accommodate in the international system. Unlike the Conservatives-Radicals Islamists, they were conciliatory in their foreign policy approach and orientation. Imam Khomeini referred to the differences between the two groups as 'two schools of thought'. Hashemi Rafsanjani called them 'factions'.

As the supreme arbiter of the Iranian affairs, Imam Khomeini can be called neither the Radicals nor the Moderates. There are two major reasons for this. First, due to fluidity of the Iranian factional politics, he looked after Iran's overall interests by performing the role of balancer, throwing his weight behind one faction or another, depending on the circumstances. Second, his entire career as the leader of the Islamic opposition to the Shah's regime and as the Supreme Leader of the Islamic Republic since 1979 revealed a complex mixture of his idealism and realism in his leadership that was difficult for the Westerners to understand. Imam Khomeini himself kept changing his line according to circumstances. Now Ayatollah Khamenei has been playing the same role as his predecessor, Ayatollah Khomeini.

Imam Khomeini as the Supreme Leader of Iran had played the central role in determining foreign policy. All his actions had intended at the fundamental goal of Iran's independence under a Faqih-ruled Islamic Republic. According to him, the first requirement of Iran's independence, is, 'intellectual independence', which required, among other things, that "we should learn the good things from foreigners and reject the bad things. . ."[14] Imam Khomeini said on 27 October 1982 that Iran must end its hermit status in the world. At his initiative and with his approval, an influential leader in foreign affairs, President Khamenei, who was also chairman of the powerful Supreme Defence Council and the general secretary of the ruling Islamic Republic Party (IRP), on 30 July 1984, called Iran's new look in world affairs "an open door foreign policy".[15] He reiterated it on 6 August 1984 that a policy should involve "rational, sound and healthy relations with all countries" and aimed at serving Iran's interest and ideology.[16] He called for greater interaction between the Islamic ideology of Iran and the "ideologies and cultures" of other countries.[17] Basically, he referred to call the fusion of national interests with Islamic ideology.

However, Ayatollah Khomeini changed his views in maintaining relations with the foreign countries as situation changed. Khomeini himself said on 29 October 1984 that it is "inadmissible to common sense and humanity not to maintain relationships with other countries, since it would mean defeat, annihilation and being buried right to the end. . ."[18] He further stated on 2 November 1985 that, we do not want to live in a country which is isolated from the rest of the world. Today's Iran cannot be that way. Other countries cannot close their borders to others either; it would be irrational. Today the world is like one family, one city. In the present world circumstances we should not be isolated."[19] He stated categorically to maintain relations with other countries is compatible not only with the Islamic Prophetic Tradition, but also with the Iranian interests. Although he omitted relations with Israel, United States, and South Africa from these declarations, he drew a significant distinction among the three. He said enigmatically that Tehran possibly could establish new relations with Washington if the United States "behaves itself".[20] Even this little opening toward the United States by Imam Khomeini was unthinkable only a few years ago. This was 'the new thinking' in Iran; which Hashemi Rafsanjani called 'interdependence'. For the first time since the seizure of the US Embassy at Tehran, *Majlis* Speaker Hashemi Rafsanjani, publicly raised the questions of restoring diplomatic relations with Washington.[21] The moderates in Iran had been also seeking to improve relations with the US and prominent among them was Hashemi Rafsanjani.

Restoration of relations between Iran and the United States was likely if Hussein Ali Muntaziri-Ali Akbar Hashemi Rafsanjani coalition would have won the power struggle. Akhavi's paper "Elite Factionalism In The Islamic Republic Of Iran" (1987) points out that Hashemi Rafsanjani sought to restore relations with the United States in the 1984-1986 period but Hujjat al-Islam Ali Khamenei (Iran's current *Velayat-e Faqih*), Ayatollah Ali Mishkini (then Chairman of the Council of Experts and Friday mosque prayer leader of Qum), Hujjat al-Islam Khu'ayniha (then State Prosecutor General), Mir Hussein Mussavi (two-term Prime Minister), and others opposed.[22] As divisions in political elites on policy issues appeared in the 1980s that still persists.

The United States was seeking to maintain relations as Iran sought. The Reagan Administration sought to improve US relations with Iran by supplying arms in exchange of hostages deal. The arms deals began in 1985. Several Israeli officials and US consultants outside the government helped in persuading the senior officials of the US, and the Director General of the Central Intelligence Agency (CIA), that it might be possible to rebuild US political ties with the 'moderates' in the Iranian government, and to free American held hostages by pro-Iranian Shiite factions in Lebanon.[23] The seizure, torture, and murder of William Buckley, the CIA station chief, in Beirut on 16 March 1984, was a catalyst in US arms deals with Iran. They believed that the only way the US could recover the hostages, and generally strengthen its position in the Gulf, was to improve relations with Iran.[24] Thus, Washington was keen in maintaining relations with Tehran for political, strategic, and economic reasons.

In the process of improving Iran-US relations, Israel played a critical role. Several senior Israeli officials had long encouraged such contacts. The Reagan Administration initiated many of these contacts with a hostile Iran. At that time it was unable to carry out its arms deals with

Saudi Arabia or expand its military relations with any of the other friendly Gulf countries.[25] It is noteworthy that the Reagan Administration tried to deal with moderates in the Iranian government at a time when Iran was actively attempting to conquer Iraq and dominate the Gulf. Iran restricted its Faw offensive by launching occasional raids against tankers in Saudi and UAE waters and pressured the GCC states to end their ties to Iraq and the US. Iran's talks with the US were then conducted directly by Iran's *Majlis* Speaker Hashemi Rafsanjani, and he used a relative as a 'second channel' to deal with the US government. Iran obtained TOWs and critically needed Hawk parts from the US.[26] The Reagan Administration tried to improve its relations by supplying critically needed arms to Iran.

By 1986, Iran had received intelligence briefings from the United States on both Iraq and the Soviet Union and had taken delivery of some of 1500 TOW missiles and components for its US-built Hawk air-defence system.[27] A few days before Imam Khomeini's optimistic appraisal, the United States had secretly sent Robert C McFarlane, the former National Security Council advisor, to Tehran to urge Iran's assistance in releasing US hostages in Lebanon and to seek a broader political dialogue with the Islamic Regime.[28] Although these shifts in Iran's military and diplomatic strategy paid dividends, they strained the limits of consensus within the regime. Powerful factions in Iran opposed any apparent softening of stand and continued to view any dealings with the *"Great Shaitan"* as treasonous.[29] The US officials had arrived Tehran to meet Iranian leadership, but left without meetings.

Iraq did not know – like the rest of the world, about Iran's secret preparation of a military strike. Iran's forces crossed the Shatt al-Arab under cover of a rainstorm, broached Iraqi defences on the southern flank and landed its forces at the Iraqi port city of Faw on the night of 9 February 1986. Iraq was not able to halt Iran's invasion of Faw. By 16 February 1986, Iran occupied over 300 square miles of the Faw Peninsula although much of this was marsh land. After 17-18 February 1986, Iraq was able to deploy its air power, firepower, and armour. Iraq fought and regained some areas of the Faw Peninsula. By early March 1986, a pattern of fighting was established in Faw that continued for the rest of 1986. Iran retained about 120 square miles of the Faw Peninsula, and was able to keep its supply lines open across the Shatt al-Arab. The Faw Peninsula is a marsh land and was relatively isolated from Basra and the main roads between Iraq and Kuwait, it was still of special importance because of its impact on the Southern Gulf. The Faw Peninsula juts out between the Shatt al-Arab and the Island of Bubiyan in Kuwait.

By mid-1986, Imam Khomeini was able to assert that "there was a time when the situation was chaotic and everything was in ruins, but - thank God – everything is now proper and right . . . Domestic and international affairs are put right."[30] Iran was able to assert and consolidate its position at both war front and domestically. Nonetheless, Imam Khomeini's claim was exaggerated, but when he made that statement he knew as most of the rest of the world did not that Iran and the United States had reached to an understanding and Iran had succeeded in restoring an arms supply relationship with the United States.

The changing Khomeini's stance on foreign policy was reflection of changing domestic situations and Iran's external requirements. It did not mean that the principle of 'neither the East nor the West' was abandoned by Imam Khomeini. In order to get 'independence', Iran had rejected both Eastern and Western domination of any kind. Imam Khomeini in his statement on 3 October 1988 categorically stated that deviation from that principle would be "treachery to Islam and the Muslims."[31] But he did not spell out what principle meant. The *Majlis* Speaker, Hashemi Rafsanjani immediately added that it meant "loyalty to the goals of the Islamic Revolution, independence and negation of foreign domination."[32] In the Khomeini period, Iran's foreign policy kept changing but the regime remained suspicious of the US and the West.

The current Supreme Leader, Ayatollah Khamenei, had also played a major role in deciding Iran's foreign policy during the Khomeini period. Ali Khamenei managed the Iran-Iraq-War and he himself visited the war fronts at several occasions. While Ali Khamenei was president, he visited the war front so many times and spent time with the IRGC fighters at the front.[33] He did not only go at the war front, but also sent his sons, Mostafa and Mojtaba, to serve as fighters at the Iran-Iraq War front.[34] Ali Khamenei's visits to the war fronts and sending his own sons to the Iran-Iraq War fronts reflect his ideological commitment in the service to the dear nation.

Iran's announcement of ceasefire on 18 July 1988 had surprised not only the world but also its own people. It announced its acceptance of UN Security Council Resolution 598. As Iran announced Iran-Iraq War ceasefire, international opinion began to turn away from its long-held pro-Iraqi posture. The threat of Iranian victory with its profound consequences for the region as a whole, had disappeared, and, for a few weeks, Iraq appeared for the first time as the recalcitrant party.[35] However, Iraq accepted the announcement of Iran-Iraq-War ceasefire.

The struggle between the radicals and the moderates had been continuing in determining the policy issues. When Iran sent a low-ranking delegation to Leonid Brezhnev's funeral, or when Iran's relations with the Soviet Union appeared to be improving, the radicals strongly opposed. As a result, the Foreign Ministry sent no one to Konstantin Chernenko's funeral. As the situation changed within and beyond Iran, the Iranian leadership began to improve relations with Russia.

Behrooz observed in his work "Factionalism in Iran under Khomeini" (1991) that the Iran-Iraq War ceasefire in July 1988 added a new dimension and intensified factional conflicts.[36] The end of the Iran-Iraq War in 1988 introduced, or rather injected, Iran's foreign policy as an important source of clashes between the factions/political groups.[37] In Behrooz's belief, Iran's priorities during the Iran-Iraq War were different and foreign policy remained, for the most part, outside factional struggle. Sudden end of the Iran-Iraq War changed domestic situation rapidly and made foreign policy an important issue in factional struggles.[38] Although factional struggle over Iran's foreign policy had continued between 1979 and 1988, but remained low. After Iran-Iraq War ceasefire, the Radicals clashed with the Moderates over foreign policy and reconstruction.

The factional struggles continued over Iran's foreign policy and economic reconstruction and further intensified in 1990 and later.[39] The issue of post-war reconstruction intensified debate between the moderates and the conservatives about participation of foreign capital and technology in the Iranian economy. While leaders like Prime Minister Mir Hussein Musavi did not favour such participation, at least by some countries, others welcomed it. President Ali Khamenei said on 7 October 1988 that when

Iran faces shortages it "should use foreign resources. . . . We cannot prolong the issue of reconstruction for 100 years. . . ."[40] The *Majlis* Speaker Hashemi Rafsanjani supplemented Ali Khamenei's statement and said in late October 1988 that "we should absorb skilled manpower from abroad and programmes should be designed to encourage the return to Iran of skilled Iranians now residing abroad. . . ."[41] While the debate on economic issues intensified, Imam Khomeini's death on 3 June 1989 began political debate that further deepened. Imam Khomeini accommodated the moderates in his regime and gave important positions to them. After death of Imam Khomeini, the new leadership Seyyid Ali Khamenei as the *Vilayat-e Faqih* (the Supreme Leader) and President Hashemi Rafsanjani marginalised the moderates in the administration. As a result, political divisions deepened and its effects also appeared at the foreign policy.

In the late 1980s, several significant changes appeared for Iran, the Iran-Iraq War ceasefire 1988, demise of Imam Khomeini on 3 June 1989, and a new leadership at the helm of Tehran. As the 1990s started, many changes ushered – the end of revolutionary era, the end of confrontational foreign policy, the process of normalisation of relations with outside world, and the economic reconstruction, but whose definitive end came in 2005 with the election of a hard-line president who reverted to the revolutionary language of the 1980s.[42] Iran's foreign policy during Mahmoud Ahmedinejad underwent a substantial overhaul as a result of his tirades, his confrontational manoeuvres, and a new cadre of diplomatic officials.[43] Again Iran pursued confrontational foreign policy and issued statements against the US and Israel. The period of confrontational foreign policy continued till June 2013 presidential elections.

Mahmoud Ahmedinejad presidency (2005-2013) sought to assert Iran's foreign policy which was contrary to the previous regime. Baktiari's work "Iran's Conservative Revival" (2007) explains the assertion of the conservative factions on Iran's foreign and security policy that appeared after the victory of conservative hardliner Mahmoud Ahmedinejad in the June 2005 presidential election. Baktiari analyses the conservative hardliner Ahmedinejad's election as president in 2005 heralded assertiveness in Iran's positions regarding foreign policy and nuclear programmes.[44] As the conservatives captured power in Iran, assertion appeared in foreign policy.

Ahmedinejad's foreign policy approach was different from the previous regime, and Iran returned to the early days of the Revolution. Ahmedinejad's 'confrontational foreign policy' displeased many and delved the Islamic Republic into isolation. He issued statements against the United States and Israel. In October 2006, a conference was organised by the government and called "World Without Zionism", during which Ahmedinejad suggested that Israel should be "wiped off the map".[45] However, he continued to cultivate and flourish Iran's relations toward the east and succeeded in enhancing the Islamic Republic's ties with China, Japan, South Korea, North Korea, India, Pakistan and other countries. Iran-Russia relations expanded tremendously during the Ahmedinejad period. Iran's relations with Pakistan improved and the visits of high dignitaries to each other demonstrated upswing in ties between the two countries. Iranian foreign policy had been engaging with China and Russia for long, but the turn east received its most definitive shape under Ahmedinejad.[46] He expanded relations with the eastern countries and strengthened them.

Mahmoud Ahmedinejad and elements of the Islamic Revolutionary Guard Corps (IRGC) preferred an alliance with Russia and China against the US, where as Hashemi Rafsanjani and other moderates have long advocated for relations with the US, and Supreme Leader Ayatollah Khamenei has remained sceptical of Iran's ties with the US.[47] Division within Iran on Tehran-Washington relationship remains and the Iranian leadership is sceptical of the Islamic Republic's ties with the United States.

Mahmoud Ahmedinejad's goals and style of diplomacy were different. Ahmedinejad's populist appeals regarding domestic political issues, and loud proclamations in defence of Iran's international interests often force the hands of others throughout the political system. Ahmedinejad's speeches attracted criticism from the international community, and especially from the United States. The Conservatives-Radicals Islamists had found itself in a position of significance.

Ahmedinejad's pro-active regional policy and pursuit of nuclear programme deteriorated Iran's relations with the Arab Gulf countries. Iran's relations with Bahrain, Yemen, Lebanon, and Saudi Arabia deteriorated due to Tehran's support of Shia minorities in those countries.[48] Political developments in Lebanon worried Saudi Arabia. When the *Hizb-e Allah* and its allies withdrew support from the cabinet in Lebanon in January 2011 just one month after the beginning of the Arab Spring, precipitated the collapse of the Saeed Harrriri government. The government headed by Prime Minister Saeed Harriri, an ally of Saudi Arabia and the son of Rafik Harriri collapsed in a few months. In July 2011, Harriri resigned under pressure and was replaced by Najib Mikati, who was friendly to Iran and Syria. Saudi Arabia and its Western and Arab allies were alarmed about the rise of Iran as a regional power and its alliance with Syria and the *Hizb-e Allah*.[49] Before the start of the Arab Spring in December 2010, the alliance among Iran, Syria and *Hizb-e Allah* was deep, strong and popular. This so-called 'Axis of Resistance' took its ideological basis from the narrative of 'resistance' against Israel and the US. The triple alliance Iran-Syria-*Hizb-e Allah* has worried the Arab governments and their allies in the West. This triple alliance has provided "Iran strategic depth at the heart of the Arab world, with limited retaliatory capability against Israel. In fact, Tehran had established ... a 'Corridor of Resistance', covering Iran, Iraq, Syria, and Lebanon – a distance of some 1500 miles."[50] Thus, Iran, Syria, and the *Hizb-e Allah* alliance has remained political and strategic which serves interests to all three parties.

Ahmedinejad's supports for Palestinian causes and statements against Israel raised concerns in the West and the United States. His defiance of the West and bellicose against the United States and Israel, his stand on the nuclear and Palestinian issues raised Iran's stature, and overshadowed moderate Arab leaders' positions in the region.[51] These statements raised stature of Ahmedinejad in Iran and the Arab and earned praises of the masses.

Iran's diplomatic strategy and tactics witnessed drastic changes under Ahmedinejad leadership. Strategically, he appealed the people and their historic pride, depicted the West as a privileged club opposed to the Muslim world's scientific progress and political independence, and questioned the global power structure (e.g., the UN Security Council's composition and legitimacy of its sanctions). Tactically, he changed Iran's position from a defendant to a prosecutor. Iranian diplomats highlighted the West's own shortcomings, presented Iran's grievances against the global powers, and countered the United States' 'arrogance and hegemony'. At the same time, Ahmedinejad sought reconciliation with the United States and wrote a letter to President George W Bush in May 2006 and he again wrote a 'letter to the American people' in November the same year reflecting his new posture.

In the light of the continued US hostility towards Iran, the Conservatives-Radicals Islamists seeks that Iran must stand on its own feet and achieve technological advances on its own. Self reliance and technological independence are among the main slogans of the Conservatives-Radicals Islamists, Mahmoud Ahmedinejad, and others in this group had consistently emphasised the importance of scientific and technological achievements as a way to enhance Iran's regional and international status.[52] In their views, the West is determined to keep Iran technologically subordinate, and in so doing it creates hindrances and difficulties designed to obstruct Iranian scientific advances.

Mahmoud Ahmedinejad received praises of the Supreme Leader Ayatollah Khamenei who is the pivot in the power structure of Iran despite the fact that his presidency faced challenges on foreign policy and economic issues. Ayatollah Ali Khamenei had backed Ahmedinejad all along and found the ex-President's ideas close to his own. At the last meeting of Ahmedinejad cabinet with Ayatollah Khamenei in mid-July 2013, he praised his government for its achievements.[53] Ahmedinejad's relation with Ayatollah Khamenei had not always remained comfortable but their relationship moved on since both carry the same ideology.

Ahmedinejad was admired in the East and South, and was vilified in the North and the West. His Islamic orthodoxy, enmity towards the United States and his infamous call for wiping out Israel from the world map echoed the goals, wishes and words of Ayatollah Khomeini himself in the 1970s and 1980s. His supports of Palestinian cause, the Lebanese *Hizb-e Allah* and *Shia* factions in Iraq were part and parcel of the position taken by Iran's leaders since 1979. Confrontational foreign policy that began in the 1980s resurfaced during the Ahmedinejad Administration which strengthened the position of the Conservatives-Radicals Islamists domestically. Mahmoud Ahmedinejad has left his indelible imprint on

Iran's politics and society by adopting a different management style at home, and a defiant foreign policy towards the West.[54] He took some independent personal positions openly different from those of other government leaders.

The outcome of Ahmedinejad's approach was Iran's isolation; unlikely coalition of Sunni Arabs, Israel, the European Community and the US against Iran; the declared intention by Egypt, Jordan, and the Gulf Cooperation Council (GCC) countries to acquire civil nuclear power plants; temporary suspension of Iran in FIFA; economic sanctions; reduction of foreign trade due to economic sanctions; reduction of oil and gas supply to foreign countries; ban on international transactions of Iranian Banks; and reduction in size of external trade volume. Iran paid the price of the confrontational foreign policy and was isolated regionally and globally. Ahmedinejad's confrontational foreign policy increased Iran's civil nuclear capability, and strengthened its ties with Iraq, Syria, and *Hizb-e Allah*, but isolated regionally and globally.

Accommodation and Reconciliation in Foreign Policy

In the late 1980s several significant changes appeared. The Iran-Iraq War ceasefire, death of Ayatollah Khomeini in June 1989, and a new leadership at Tehran. As the 1990s started, many changes were witnessed in the Islamic Republic, end of the revolutionary era, the process of normalisation of relations with outside world, and the economic reconstruction. Iran's foreign policy saw perceptible shifts as the domestic political situation changed. President Hashemi Rafsanjani began the process of normalisation of relation with the outside world. Rafsanjani sought economic reconstruction which required external assistance in the forms of funds and technology. The Islamic Republic needed normalisation of relations with the outside world in order to receive foreign assistances. The process of normalisation of relations with the outside world was begun by Rafsanjani which was further continued by his successor Mohammad Khatami.

The Rafsanjani Administration (1989-97) provided opportunity and gave rise to the Moderates. Rafsanjani, the speaker of the *Majlis* and second in command in the war against Iraq realised in the mid-1980s that it could not proceed further, but he knew it was impossible to break revolutionary inertia. In order to maintain his influence, Rafsanjani wavered between the Conservatives and the Moderates groups. However, he remained soft towards the Moderates. His foreign policy approach suited the Moderates Islamists, but his domestic policy remained favourable to the Conservatives.

The Rafsanjani Administration pursued moderation in foreign policy and sought engagement with the outside world. The Moderates Islamists had their greatest impact in the area of foreign policy.[55] Members of this faction had been instrumental in developing ties towards Central Asia and the Caucasus region and enhancing trade relations with the West.[56] President Rafsanjani tried to improve relations with the West and the US but faced obstacles. Ayatollah Khomeini's *fatwa* of death sentence against Salman Rushdie's *The Satanic Verses* in February 1989 remained a major obstacle in improving Iran's relation with the West. Iranian leadership did not want to withdraw Ayatollah Khomeini's *fatwa* against Rushdie as the West sought, and the Rushdie affair remained a contentious issue between Iran and the West relationship.[57] The Conservatives-Radicals Islamists objected closer relations with the West, especially the United States.[58] The *Majlis* still remained an obstacle in improving Iran's relations with the West.[59] President Rafsanjani's attempt to improve ties with the West was a major foreign policy objective which was obstructed by the Conservatives-Radicals. Nonetheless, this faction partially succeeded in thwarting Rafsanjani's move. Rafsanjani succeeded to some extent in improving ties with the West which had disarrayed during the 1980s.

The Clinton Administration's 'Dual Containment' policy did not go well in Tehran where the Rafsanjani Administration sought engagement with the foreign countries including the United States. The US policy strengthened views of the Conservative-Radicals Islamists over which they had been arguing for long. They argued that Iran should not extend help to the foreigners since the results would be negative. However, struggle continued between the Conservatives-Radicals Islamist and the Moderates Islamists in determining foreign policy orientations and goals during the Rafsanjani period.

Mohammad Khatami called for the reduction on international tension through dialogue and declared during his presidential elections campaigns for devotion to a "detente with the outside world".[60] He sought to establish relations with the outside world based on national "principles and values".[61] Mohammad Khatami's detente policy stressed to defuse tension with the outside world, and establish normal relations with all countries on the basis of mutual respect and equality. Khatami politically, intellectually and temperamentally harboured an enlightened and pragmatic attitude and outlook toward the outside world. He tacitly rejected the conservative views of 'Western cultural onslaught' and regarded Western civilisation as intellectually, ethically, technologically and politically. In his view, misunderstandings, disputes, and quarrels with other nations should be resolved not by war, but through dialogue and negotiations. Iran was isolated in the world community when he assumed office in 1997. Khatami took measures to end the mutual distrust with the regional countries and beyond. A tenuous relationship with the European Union, suspicion by Sunni Muslim countries regarding Iran's propagation of *Shiism* in the region (e.g., Bahrain, Saudi Arabia, and Lebanon), some disputes with neighbours (e.g., Pakistan, Turkey, Azerbaijan, the Taliban's Afghanistan, and the United Arab Emirates), and a peace treaty with Iraq were all formidable challenges to his foreign policy agenda.

Khatami started his diplomatic maneuvours with following the Supreme Leader's tripartite principles based on 'dignity, rationality, and national interests'. He initiated rapprochement with Saudi Arabia and succeeded in melting suspicion that emerged in the 1980s and 1990s. Iran's relations with other Arab countries in the Persian Gulf and the region (e.g., Bahrain, Qatar, the UAE, and Iraq) improved. Ties with Pakistan and Turkey improved and strengthened. Friendship with China and Russia intensified. Traditional closeness with the EU, which had been disarrayed, was restored. The acceptance by the United Nations of his suggestion to declare 2001 the year of 'Dialogue among Civilisations', was a notable diplomatic success.

Iran's relations with the outside world improved during the Khatami Administration. When Khatami was elected as president, Iran had Syria as its only friend in the Arab world. Pakistan officially represented Iran's diplomatic interests in Washington, but maintained a tense tie with Tehran. Iran maintained trade relations with the EU. Iran's relations with Russia and china had improved and became comfortable. The US and Israel were the only declared enemies. By the end of Khatami's tenure, Cuba, North Korea, and Venezuela had joined Russia and China in Iran's steady supports against the US. Afghanistan and Iraq had better relations with Iran despite the presence of the US forces. However, Khatami's foreign policy initiatives in the region proved to be short-lived. Agreement on the division of the Caspian Sea resources did not materialise despite negotiations and conferences among the littoral states. Ties with the UAE and Turkey remained strained.

Iran-EU conflict intensified when it was discovered that Iran had clandestinely engaged in an uranium enrichment process. Khatami's strong stance on Iran's rights under the NTP to engage in uranium conversion for peaceful purposes, and his firm resistance to the demands and offers by the US-EU, halted normalisation of the Iran-EU relations, and forced the EU trio to side with the US.[62] After statement of President Bush on Iran's nuclear programme as 'unacceptable', a British-French-German effort began to convince Tehran to freeze sensitive nuclear programme in exchange of economic, security, and technological incentives.

While Khatami had been facing serious challenges on Iran's nuclear issues and relations with EU were deteriorating, he agreed on a deal with the EU-trio (Britain, France, and Germany). Iran signed a nuclear deal in 2003-2004 with Britain, France, and Germany for temporary voluntarily suspension of its nuclear activities with additional protocol to defuse tension between Iran and EU-trio since the US and EU-trio views seemed converged. The deal did not go well within political establishment in Tehran. Ayatollah Khamenei, the Supreme Leader, did not endorse such deal but remained silent.

Ayatollah Khamenei carries numerous features in his personality. He hides his views and policies. He rarely issues statements on sensitive issues. The secret nature of Khamenei's real views and policy preferences has confused his supporters and rivals within the political establishment and outside. It actually comes into light much later, what his policy preferences were? Ayatollah Khamenei's view to the nuclear agreements with the EU-3 (Britain, France, and Germany) and the Atomic Energy Agency (IAEA) in 2003-2004 on accepting the Additional Protocols and temporary suspension of uranium enrichment by the Khatami Administration were understood as his support for these agreements. In 2012, he strongly condemned the reformists (Khatami faction) and moderates (Rafsanjani faction) for those agreements. Only after sidelining the reformists and moderates, and replacing them with the hard-line Mahmoud Ahmedinejad, he revealed his views and policy preferences. The political players such as Rafsanjani and the reformists explicitly state their views on policy issues, but Ayatollah Khamenei did not reveal his objectives and preferences. This has been reflecting in pursuit of his foreign policy.

Mohamad Khatami started to issue conciliatory statements toward the US immediately after assuming presidency. He began to reiterate the longstanding official line that relations between the countries should be based on mutual respect, common interest, and non-interference in each other's internal affairs, free from domination and hegemony, and recognition of Iran's independence, sovereignty, and equality of status. In a press conference at the time of the OIC meeting in Tehran in December 1997, he expressed hope for a philosophical and historical change with American people. In an interview with CNN on 8 January 1998, he expressed desire to open a new chapter between the two countries.[63] Khatam's interview with the CNN on January 1998 is a significant occasion of 'dialogue among civilisations' in the context of international relations.[64] In June 1998, both President Clinton and Secretary of State Albright made encouraging statements. In March 2000, Secretary of State, Albright, deplored Washington's role in the 1953 Anglo-American coup against Mussadeq's elected government. Iran also wished to improve Tehran-Washington relationship and provided logistic and intelligence supports to the US against the Taliban regime during US attacks against the Taliban government in Afghanistan in 2001. The earlier efforts to improve ties between the two countries became futile when President George W Bush placed Iran on the "axis of evil" along with Iraq and North Korea in January 2002. Meanwhile sanctions against Iran continued.

The conduct of foreign policy and statements of American leaders towards Iran have significantly influenced the positions and the relative strengths and agendas of each of the Iranian factions.[65] When President Bush categorised Iran a member of an 'Axis of Evil' in January 2002 the Moderates-Reformists Islamists went into defensive and sought improvement in Iran-US relations. The US posture towards Iran after its invasion over Iraq in 2003 and afterwards became increasingly confrontational. The US hinted its desire to initiate 'regime change' in Iran and openly declared that 'all options are on the table' to deal with 'Iranian threat', which did not go well in Iran. This bellicose posture helped in strengthening the Conservative-Radical Islamists within the Iranian regime.[66] The behaviour and attitude of the foreign powers towards Iran significantly contributed in shaping Iranian domestic politics.

The Khatami Administration's rapprochement with the outside world was always effectively undermined by the difficulties of engagement with the United States and continued hostility toward Israel. Iran's hostility toward the US and Israel had its origin in Ayatollah Khomeini's writings and foreign policy speeches regarding Zionism and, and the necessity of following a 'Neither East Nor West' foreign policy. Hashemi Rafsanjani had sought friendship with the East (Russia and China) to counter Washington's dual containment policy.

Iran's relations with the Gulf countries deteriorated due to its pro-active Gulf policy and its growing influence in the post-Saddam Iraq. As Saddam Hussein was removed by the US-led coalitions in 2003, sectarian conflict ensued in Iraq and intensified in later days which still continue. The post-Saddam period marked the rise of sectarian clashes in Iraq and in the region. By the end of the tenure of the Khatami presidency, Iran's influence tremendously increased in Iraq, employed all means political, diplomatic, economic, security, intelligence, social, cultural, religious to enhance its presence and influence in Iraq. Iran and Iraq signed security, political, economic, social, and cultural pacts. Iran's growing relations with Iraq did not go well in the Arab governments. Iran's relations with Pakistan and India improved. The Khatami Administration succeeded in changing Iran's image from an unfriendliness nation in the international community to a benign, positive and accommodative nation. But, by the end of Khatami's tenure, Iran's relations with the Arab governments began to deteriorate which further deteriorated during the Ahmedinejad presidency 2005-2013, and tensions increased.

President Rouhani: Continuity and Change

Unlike Mohammad Khatami's liberal-pragmatist view and Mahmoud Ahmedinejad's ideological populist stance, President Rouhani is bent to pursue a centrist-moderate agenda. His election campaign of the June 2013 reflected such a vision: Iran should engage in serious negotiations with the West, reduce regional conflict, and prioritise its economic recovery above its nuclear programme. Will Rouhani be able to implement his vision, considering the structural, institutional, and strategic hurdles to his success? President Rouhani has evolved his policy preferences to suit the changing international system. For instance, he seeks engagements with the outside world in view of changing international system.

International system has been changing. The pattern of interactions among the nation-states has been changing too. Collective action and cooperation has become the hallmarks of the era. Multilateralism, the collective search for common solutions to common problems is desirable at both the regional and global levels. Even world major powers have learned that they can no longer pursue their interests or achieve their particular goals unilaterally. Wilful cooperation has gradually developed as a new working pattern of interaction among states and it has been replacing the once predominant and now discredited pattern of confrontation, unconditional subservience, and continued rivalry.

In the changing pattern of interactions, unilateral policy of the global major powers has been losing relevance. The global major powers have been facing challenges in implementation of their unilateral policies since pattern of interaction has been changing. Iran's Foreign Minister, Mohammad Javad Zarif, under Rouhani Administration cryptically criticised the US and the West for imposing their views on other nations and taking measures to contain and obstruct other countries' development. He observed:

"globalisation and the ensuing rise of collective action and cooperative approaches, the idea of seeking or imposing zero-sum games have lost its lust. Still, some actors cling to their old habits and habitually pursue their own interests at the expense of others. The insistence of some major powers on playing zero-sum games with win-lose outcomes has usually led to lose-lose outcomes for all the players involved."[67]

The world major powers should consider and respect views and opinions of the other countries in dealing disputes and conflicts. Unilateral policy may escalate conflicts and disputes.

As policy preferences, President Rouhani seeks to reduce tensions with the US and European countries. He has been engaged in negotiations with the P5+1 (France, Britain, US, China and Russia, plus Germany) to find common ground and reach an agreement to break impasse on its nuclear dispute.[68] At the same time, President Rouhani seeks to preserve Iran's scientific achievement, honour Iran's inalienable right under the NPT, and to end the sanctions that have been imposed by the world powers.

Rouhani has called for 'prudent moderation'. This vision aims to move Iran away from confrontation and towards dialogue and constructive engagement in order to minimise threats and maximise national security, elevate Iran's stature, and achieve long-term comprehensive development. 'Prudent moderation' is an approach which is based on realism, realistic assessment of international system, and constructive engagement. Rouhani's constructive engagement is based on dialogue and interaction with other countries on an equal footing with mutual respect and shared interests. Realism requires an understanding of the nature, order, structure, mechanism, and power dynamics of the international system and of the potential, and limits of its institutions. Rouhani pursues moderation after evaluation of Iran's actual capacities, capabilities, and constraints. Rouhani's approach reflects a delicate balancing act between national, regional, and global needs, on the one hand, and the available means, instruments, and policies, on the other; between continuity and change in foreign policy; between goals and means; and among various powers in a dynamically changing world.

Iran's foreign policy under Rouhani is based on achieving understanding and consensus at domestic level and constructive engagement and effective cooperation with the outside world. The Islamic Republic's policies will be guided by the principles of dignity, rationality, and prudence. Iran will expand and deepen its bilateral and multilateral relations through engagement with various states and world organisations. Under the Rouhani Administration multilateralism plays a central role in Iran's external relations. First, Iran is involved globally in a coalitions of like-minded states and promotes peace and stability; second, it also involves in defending individual and collective rights of Iranian nationals everywhere and promotes Iranian-Islamic culture, the Persian language, Islamic values and Islamic democracy as a form of governance; and third, it continues to support the cause of oppressed people across the world, especially in Palestine, and rejects Zionist encroachments in the Muslim world.[69] It reflects from Rouhani's policy that he has pursued continuity and change in the realm of foreign policy.

Iran's foreign policy priority is to improve its relations with the world and immediate neighbours. It appears from Rouhani's policies that Iran prudently manages its ties with the United States by containing existing disagreements and preventing further tensions from emerging, and gradually easing tensions. Moreover, The Islamic Republic seeks deep interacts with the European countries and other Western states in order to expand relations. Under Rouhani Iran seeks to expand and consolidate its amicable ties with other major powers, like China, India, and Russia.[70] President Rouhani continues the previous government's 'look east policy' that stressed expansion of ties with China, India and Russia. Actually, it is a continuation of the Conservatives-Radicals' 'look east policy' to counter the West.

It appears that the Rouhani Administration's foreign policy approach provides opportunity to other states for a close interaction with the Islamic Republic. The current dispensation has its own constrains and challenges. Iran's Foreign Minister Mohammad Javad zarif states:

> "it is imperative for other states to accept the reality of Iran's prominent role in the Middle East and beyond and to recognise and respect Iran's

legitimate national rights, interests, and security concerns. It is equally important for other states to scrupulously observe the sensitivities of the Iranian nation, particularly its national dignity, independence, and achievements. Westerners, especially Americans, need to modify their understandings of Iran and the Middle East and develop a better grasp of the region's realities, avoiding the analytic and practical mistakes of the past. Courage and leadership are required to seize this historic opportunity, which might not come again. The opportunity must not be lost."[71]

Visibly the Rouhani Administration provides opportunity to the foreign countries for a close interaction with the Islamic Republic. Thus, Iran seeks to break isolation since its economy has been seriously suffering due to sanctions.

The Arab Spring and Iran's Policy

Since early 2011 political upheavals in the Arab world and their generally bloody outcomes – dubbed by some as 'the Arab Spring' and by others a 'the Islamic Awakening' – have introduced another destabilising factor to the region. The trends appear likely to continue for some time, but the directions of the process are uncertain. Iran enthusiastically supported the uprisings in Tunisia, Egypt, Libya, and Bahrain, dubbing them as the 'Islamic Awakening' inspired by its own Islamic Revolution 1979. The Arab Spring also arrived in Syrian in 2011 and took gradually violent shape. The Syrian crisis is deeply felt by Iran since the two countries have been maintaining friendly relations. Iran has been facing serious challenges on Syria issue both internally and externally. The Islamic Republic feels challenges internally due to domestic political dynamics. Externally, Iran faces challenges on Syria issue from some regional countries such as Saudi Arabia, Qatar, and Turkey and global powers as the US and its Western allies.

While the Arab Spring reached Syria in February 2011, Iran changed its tone. Iran rallied behind Syria when anti-regime demonstrations broke in February 2011.[72] Iran pledged to boost bilateral trade and investment as a way to help the Syrian government in tackling growing popular discontent and welcomed the nominal reforms which were introduced by President Bashar al-Assad in March and April 2011, as significant steps in the right direction. Iranian officials visited Syria and assured President Bashar al-Assad to assist him.

Although Syrian uprising was initially peaceful and democratic, Iran condemned it as a conspiracy concocted by the US and Israel to overthrow Bashr Al-Assad and eliminate the 'Axis of resistance'. Initially, Iran believed that Assad will suppress the uprising. As uprising progressed, Syria faced serious problems in containing it. The *Hizb-e Allah* has supported Syria with arms and manpower in suppressing the uprising, but it still continues. Iran has been supporting Bashr Al-Assad in Syria due to varieties of reasons, and considers Syria as a friend and ally in the region. In the 1980s, only Syria and Libya supported Iran while later was isolated regionally and globally in the aftermath of the Revolution of 1979. Iran has extended moral, political, diplomatic and economic supports, including arms and military personnel to Syria. Iranian military specialists have visited Syria to advise Syrian military and Iranian military personnel have been involved in fighting along the Syrian military to suppress rebels.[73] Iran has supplied arms to bolster Syria's military offensive capability.[74] By supporting Bashr Al-Assad, Iran has fallen into a trap from which it cannot escape without substantial political and economic costs.[75] The violence and resurgence in Syria can be seen in the larger context since such anti-government activities continue in some countries in the region, and they are ideologically motivated. Such continued violence and extremism has adversely affected regional security and stability. Regional rivals have played significant roles for disturbances and clashes in Yemen, Syria, Iraq, and Lebanon. Saudi Arabia claims Iranian connections to anti-government protests in Bahrain, and Riyadh similarly blames Tehran of supporting Houthi rebels against the Yemeni government.[76] The clashes have escalated social conflicts, and it may lead to the break up of a country on sectarian ground. The continued violence has endangered regional peace and stability.

At the beginning of the Syrian uprising in 2011, there were moderate voices in the Islamic Republic who called for a policy change towards Syria. They believed that Bashr Al-Assad has lost legitimacy because of his ruthless suppression of the people and urged Tehran to gradually distance itself from Assad regime and instead support the uprising. In their view, Iran has no vital interests in Syria, and backing Assad would place Iran on the wrong side of history, exposing its hypocrisy for supporting every other Arab uprising but what about Syria.[77] The Conservatives-Radicals, who controlled Iranian foreign policy till the June 2013 presidential elections believed that supporting Assad was a moral responsibility as well as national security imperative. They argued in favour of Bash Al-Assad since he opposes the US and Israel, and strongly supports to the Palestinians and their resistance.

The Conservatives-Radicals has linked Syria to Iranian national security interest and argued that a hostile government in Damascus would make it easier for Israel to attack the *Hizb-e Allah* and then Iran.[78] Ali Akbar Velayati, ex-Foreign Minister of Iran and a senior advisor to Ayatollah Ali Khamenei, declared that "Syria is the golden ring of the chain of resistance against Israel that must be protected."[79] Syria offers Iran a strategically located platform from which to penetrate in the region and pressure Israel. Bashr al-Assad's survival allows Iran access to Syria as a platform from which to project its influence in the region.[80] Syria has been continuously debated in Iran's foreign policy circle and religious community. One influential cleric claimed that Syria has a strategic significance for the Islamic Republic like that of Iran's own oil-rich province of Khuzestan.[81] Domestically, the Conservatives-Radicals and Moderates-Reformists are divided and each is pulling in opposite direction over Syria issue.

From the very beginning, Iran's Supreme Leader, Ayatollah Khamenei, is determined to support Assad in Syria. Actually, for years he has been personally engaged in making strategy in this area. While he became the Supreme Leader after demise of Ayatollah Khomeini, Nasrallah asked him to appoint a personal representative to manage Iran's involvement in the region as Khomeini did earlier, but Khamenei said no, and reminded him that he was responsible for managing Israel and Lebanon. Ayatollah Khamenei has been personally managing the region around Syria since 1980 which is connected to Israel. In his belief, if Assad is overthrown, it would embolden the US to engineer regime change in Tehran. In Khamenei's view, if one part of the Syria-Iran-Hizbeallah alliance is weakened or destroyed, the other two would irrevocably suffer, and Assad seems to have the same mindset.[82] Thus, the Conservatives-Radicals have been extending full support to Bashr al-Assad in Syria.

The Islamic Republic has been actively involved in Syria and the US inaction in Syria has surprised Tehran. The US inaction in Syria is meant that "Washington has treated the Syrian conflict as regional issue and an unwelcome part of the Saudi-Iranian cold war."[83] This has meant that Iran is in a position in which its limited investment has not been challenged militarily. Syria has also got support from Russia and China that has provided a comfortable situation for Iran to support Syria. Tehran had earlier been in bind to defend the Assad regime in Syria, "but now find itself not running any substantial risks or paying a high price for its involvement."[84] The US inaction in Syria has antagonised some Arab countries such as Saudi Arabia, Turkey, and Qatar since they are a close ally of the US and seek to overthrow Bashr al-Assad in Syria. The US inaction in Syria is interpreted by some Arab countries as a sign of growing Tehran-Washington relations.

Economic Sanctions Impact over Foreign Policy

The Revolution of 1979 deteriorated Iran's relations with the United States, European and other countries. As Iran's relations with the outside world deteriorated, its economy had faced serious challenges and suffered. The US and the European countries imposed economic sanctions against Iran that had negative effects over the Iranian economy. The Khomeini regime moved decisively to balance Iran's relations between the East and the West. As soon as the West European countries lifted economic sanctions against Iran after the settlement of the hostage dispute in January 1981, mutual economic and commercial ties swiftly expanded. Japan and West Germany again became Iran's trading partners. Even before the Iran-Iraq War ceasefire, more that 70 percent of Iran's total imports in 1983-84 came from Canada, Japan, and Western Europe, and more than 50 percent of its total exports went to these same areas.[85] By comparison, in the same year only 10 percent of Iran's imports came from Eastern Europe and the Soviet Union, and only 26 percent of its exports went to the Soviets.

Iran's confrontational foreign policy and its behaviour with the outside world caused economic sanctions against it.[86] Iran's behaviour has been depicted as a threat to the US interests and to those of the international community. The US action against Iran as 'dual containment' in 1992 and trade embargo policies had been seen as the protection of the US national interest, defined as the development of a stable, peaceful environment in the Gulf region. The Iranian economy has been operating since 1979 under economic and political pressures of one kind or another. The economic sanctions against Iran till the Iran-Iraq War ceasefire in 1988 coincided with the fall of oil prices in the world market that caused in reduction of oil revenues. The average rate of decline in GDP between 1984-85 and 1988-89 was about 2 percent a year, but this decline was both due to fall in the annual value of oil exports in that period and economic sanctions. The post-war period also came under intense US economic sanctions. Other countries refrained to interact with Iran due to US pressures, and avoided to invest in Iran.

The US sanctions caused difficulties for Iranian economy. The US 'dual containment' policy in 1992 and economic sanction caused trade problems. The immediate effect of US President Bill Clinton's Executive Order of 8 May 1995, banning trade and investment with Iran, resulted in a sudden plunge in the value of the Iranian currency. This US economic sanction further created difficulties for the Iranian economy since the foreign entities could not invest in Iran's energy sector. Since then, sales contracts with non-American oil customers, such as the Chinese, Italian, French, Spanish and Portugese have been signed, but only by offering some discounts. In 1995, the temporary storing of Iranian crude in large oil tankers in search of new buyers caused storage costs.

The French oil company, Total, SA, replaced CONOCO for the development of the Sirri offshore oil fields in the Persian Gulf (after CONOCO's deal was cancelled under the May 1995 sanction), the new agreement was more limited and less lucrative for Iran. US sanctions against Iran have had impact in other areas as well. The Dutch/Shell group avoided signing contracts with Iran due to US opposition. In 1995, China's decision to freeze the release of loan to Iran ($450 million) for the construction of the Godar-e Landar dam on the Karun river was taken because of US pressure. In September 1995, China suspended an agreement to provide Iran with two 300-MW nuclear reactors. China, in November 1995, announced the cancellation of the sale of a uranium conversion facility to Iran due to US pressure.

Sanctions and the US pressures continued throughout the 1990s and thereafter, but Mohammad Khatami managed Iranian economy and growth rate increased. According to official data, real gross domestic product (GDP) rose to an average growth rate of 4.6 percent a year from 1997 to 2005.[87] This growth was registered despite low oil prices, drought, and other unfavourable elements in the first three years of the Khatami Administration. Iran's income from oil exports increased from $15.4 billion in 1997 to $36.3 billion in 2005 because of surge in crude oil prices. Non-oil exports increased from $2.9 billion to $7.5 billion. Exports of services rose from less than $1 billion to nearly $3 billion.

Iranian economy's dependency on oil exports continued and Khatami could not manage economy as expected. The budget reliance on oil income rose from 42 percent to 63 percent during his presidency.[88] The budget deficit increased from 6 percent to 16 percent.[89] The value of rial was depreciated. Mohammad Khatami tried to improve Iranian economy and took various measures for it. The Khatami presidency changed some economic policies and encouraged privatisation of public enterprises. A National Privatisation Organisation was set up in early 2001 to centralise, coordinate, and efficiently conduct the government's privatisation policy.[90] Khatami encouraged the domestic and foreign private entities to invest in Iran. However, Iran's economic performances were not satisfactory during the Khatami period.

Iran's annual growth rate declined during the Ahmedinejad presidency. The report of the Central Bank of Iran shows that the annual GDP growth rate in the first year of Ahmedinejad's presidency declined from 7.1 percent in the first quarter of 21 March - 21 June 2005 to 4.7 in the first quarter of 21 March - 21 June 2006. Slack in domestic and foreign investments, stagnant factor in productivity and reduced global competitiveness caused the decline. Private domestic investments – particularly in the industrial and construction sectors – reduced because of several reasons: business uncertainties increased due to Ahmedinejad's statements on economic issues such as stock market speculation and wealth accumulation, government's discouragement policies towards private sectors and Ahmedinejad's defiant and bellicose on foreign policy and nuclear issue. In early October 2006, Japan's Inpex gave up its leading role in the $2 billion development of Iran's Azadegan oil field contracted in 2004.[91] Iran's energy sector has been continuously facing sanctions since 1994. The Islamic Republic has been under comprehensive sanctions since the late 2000s targeting energy sector. As a result, new projects have either been delayed or developed at a lower space than the actual plan, since several international oil companies have suspended operations.[92] Iran's natural gas sector has also been hampered by international sanctions.

The United Nations Conference on Trade and Development's 2006 annual report shows the total FDI figure for Iran in 2005 as only $30 million – a 70 percent decline from the UNCTD 2004 data against $76 million of capital outflow.[93] The Iranian government sources refute these figures. Foreign private sources invested $1.15 billion in 2005 and about $800 million in 2006 – less than the $4.26 billion in 2004.[94] The private sector was discouraged by the Ahmedinejad Administration. The private entities had little invested due to Ahmedinejad's economic policy and his confrontational foreign policy.

Ahmedinejad kept the Iranian rial artificially high against the US dollar and other foreign exchange to alleviate economic difficulties. This policy brought several consequences for the Iranian economy: reduced domestic producers' ability to compete with foreign suppliers; brought down domestic production capacity of import-competing industries; increased unemployment because of imports; deteriorated Iran's non-oil trade balance; and gave a hefty subsidy to foreign farmers and manufacturers. The over-valued exchange rate also increased on Iranian economy's dependence on the world economy and capital flight. With imposition of sanctions by UN Security Council on Iran's oil exports and its Central Bank operation in 2011, the Iranian rial lost two-thirds of its value against the dollar and other foreign exchanges.

Ahmedinejad's confrontational foreign policy brought pressure over Iranian economy. It has reflected in the Iranian economic indicators. The

GDP growth of 6.9 percent in 2005 gradually declined year after year, ending the last two years of the Ahmedinejad Administration (2011 and 2012) in negative figures, at minus 1.7 percent and minus 5.4 percent respectively.[95] However, the GDP growth rate during whole Ahmedinejad period shows at an average annual growth of 3 percent. Iran received nearly $ 700 billion as oil-export revenue during Ahmedinejad presidency (2005-2013) and around $ 440 billion was spent on imports, raised yearly purchases from $36 billion to $60billion.

Mahmoud Ahmedinejad tried to improve Iran' economy but faced several challenges. Ahmedinejad's confrontational policy with the US, the European Union and the United Nations, triggered one economic sanction after another.[96] They imposed economic and political sanctions against Iran which still exist. Iran's trade with foreign countries has suffered. Particularly, the energy sector has suffered immensely. The banking sector has also suffered. However, they have partially lifted sanctions under the November 2013 and July 2015 nuclear agreements between Iran and P5+1. But the major sanctions still continue. Iran's behaviour under Ahmedinejad presidency underwent changes, consequently economic relationship and trade were adversely affected.

Economic sanctions were imposed against Iran during the Ahmedinejad period by the US, EU, and the UN Security Council that caused economic hardship to people. Ayatollah Khamenei accused the US on Iran's economic sanctions while he was speaking in the north-eastern city of Mashhad on 21 March 2015 that the US is using economic pressure to turn Iranians against the Islamic rule, where people chanted "Death to America". Ayatollah Khamenei continued: "Of course yes, death to America, because America is the original source of this pressure. They insist on putting pressure on our dear people's economy. What's their goal? Their goal is to put the people against the system."[97] Ayatollah Khamenei's acceptance of economic difficulties reflects that leadership has felt economic sanctions as cause of economic hardship to people. It appears that Iran started negotiations with the P-5 +1 on its nuclear dispute because of economic sanctions. Thus, Iran has modified its posture due to economic pressure.

Economic sanctions caused shortages of essential commodities in Iran. Replacing imports from the US had to be done at higher prices or less desirable substitutes, in third-party markets. Renovating the aging, US-based, oil infrastructure has been expensive. Iran's defence purchase ability has been curtailed due to sanctions. Despite economic sanctions, Iran has obtained arms and ammunitions from China, Russia, North Korea, and other sources.

In nutshell, the majority of bilateral oil and gas agreements involving capital investment or transfer of technology have been effectively blocked by sanctions and US pressures. US sanctions have changed the situation for Iranian business by adversely affecting the country's terms of trade and raising the cost of foreign capital for development financing. Moreover, Iran's defence agreements and transfers of sensitive technology with other countries are also blocked by sanctions and US pressures.

Is there any chance that Iran will modify its behaviour under the UN, the US, and the European Union sanctions? The answer will depend on the outcome of the balance between two countervailing forces in Iran: increasing economic hardships and deprivations caused by sanctions which could weaken the regime's hold on its power; and rising nationalistic fervour and religious solidarity that could strengthen the regime's legitimacy and political bases of power. It is noteworthy that sanctions raised nationalistic fervour, strengthened the regime's legitimacy and increased power bases. It has been also seen that sanctions helped in modifying Iran's political posture to some extent. In a nutshell, sanctions help/helped in strengthening regime's legitimacy and modify political posture to some extent.

It has been seen when external forces applied sanctions and created difficulties for the Iranian economy and posed challenges for the regime, Iran changed its behaviour. But it also served to keep the regime in power beyond its time. Universal enmity may have the unintended consequence of arousing the people's sense of patriotism where survival at any cost may become a stronger instinct. Any declared intention to isolate and destabilise Iran is played into the *ulema's* hands, and strengthened nationalistic sentiments and solidarity.

In the 1980s when the people felt economic hardship, Iran changed its behaviour. Imam Khomeini modified the country's external behaviour and opened Iran's relations with foreign countries. Ahmedinejad's policy caused sanctions and consequently Iranian economy suffered. President Rouhani seeks engagement with the outside world to ease sanctions and avoid economic hardship. Apparently, the changes in Iran's behaviour seem to break international isolation and avoid economic difficulties. Economic hardship may become a deciding factor in changing Iran's behaviour only when nationalistic elements within the politically active population are convinced that Iran's territorial integrity and sovereignty will not suffer by the sanctions and the US enmity.

Political Factions Struggle over Foreign Policy

The factional struggle over foreign policy has been seen since the Iranian Revolution 1979. The Conservatives-Radicals Islamists coalition has generally prevailed over the Moderates-Reformists Islamists coalition since its entrenched penetration and influence in system. They differ over self-reliant independence vs. integration into the world.[98] Both groups are sharply divided over Iran's integration into the world system. At both domestic and foreign relations issues, "the US-led efforts aimed at curbing both Iran's regional influence and its nuclear programme, often play determining roles in forcing the hands of one faction over another or, at times, even marginalising one or more factions to the benefits of others."[99] The foreign countries' policies against Iran restrict others factions to openly express their views on foreign policy and security issues and even marginalise them in the system. For Moderates Islamists, economic development, modernisation, national wealth, access to international technology, health, education, efficiency, and globalisation were considered the concerns of the state. The Conservatives-Radicals Islamists considered history a struggle against imperialism and adherence to a code of ethical conduct as pressing issues. From Conservatives-Radicals perspective, there was no need to extend help to foreigners. In the end, Iran did not achieve any result by cooperating with the British, Russians and Americans. The international order is based on oppression, conspiracy and anti-Islamic sentiment.

In addition, the Conservatives-Radicals Islamists believes in the preservation of the ideological order, the clerical establishment and state control of culture, and considers the Western world as Iran's enemy. However, the Moderates-Reformists do not disassociate the domestic structure from global dynamics, national economy from foreign policy and national security from economic development. The Conservatives-Radicals Islamists believes that Iran should focus on domestic agendas and maintain a calculated distance from the international community. The Moderates-Reformists believe that Iran should join the WTO and become a normal member of the international community. The Conservatives-Radicals Islamists asserts that Iran's security is guaranteed when it disassociated itself from the political and economic impositions of the international capitalist system led by the US. The Moderates-Reformists presume that Iran's national security stems from its economic interdependence with the international community, and Iran should focus on producing national wealth, economic diplomacy and soft politics. Whereas the threat perceptions of the Conservatives-Radicals Islamists are fundamentally military and existential, the Moderates-Reformists perceive economic, soft-power issues as basic threats to the state.

The Moderates-Reformists believe that Iran cannot shape the regional order, but has capability to exhaust counter-players. The primary reason for this is its detachment from great powers and its continuing frictions with Arab governments. The Conservatives-Radicals seek to break status quo and they pursue revisionist foreign policy. They are divided on foreign policy issues such as Iraq, Syria, Iran's role in the Persian Gulf and in the larger West Asia, Iran's ties with *Hamas* and *Hizb-e Allah*, and Iran's relations with the US.

Of these issues, there is only consensus between the two camps over the *Hizb-e Allah*, which both sides see as legitimate organisation that is rightfully engaged in a struggle for the protection of Lebanese Shiites and other from Israeli attacks. The threat of Israel is real and constant and the *Hizb-e Allah* is required to remain there. Iran considers the *Hizb-e Allah* as its strategic depth in the Arab world and could be used against Israel and the US when they would issue threat to Tehran. Iran and Syria both have helped the *Hizb-e Allah* materially and financially. The 2006 summer conflict between Israel and *Hizb-e Allah* clearly demonstrated the *Hizb-e Allah's* military capabilities. It could not have achieved without foreign support from both Tehran and Damascus.

As far as Hamas is concerned the two camps agreed within the broader context of the Palestine-Israel conflict. Neither camp recognises Israel. The Moderates-Reformists Islamists coalition, however, does not openly advocate destruction of Israel. President Hashemi Rafsanjani and his Foreign Minister Ali Akbar Velayati in the late 1980s and early 1990s even went so far to maintain that Iran would not oppose to a mutually satisfactory resolution to the Israeli-Palestinian conflict.[100] Mohammad Khatami did not issue statements against Israel and sought reconciliation with the West. The Rouhani Administration has also remained cautious in issuing statements regarding Israel and seeks to maintain status quo in the region. It seems that the moderates have realised reality of the region.

For the Conservatives-Radicals Islamists, even a de facto acknowledgement of Isreal's right to exist is tantamount to a betrayal of the Palestinian cause. In their view, the solution of the Palestinian-Israeli conflict involves only one state, a Palestine one and Hamas is the rightful heir to that state. President Ahmedinejad issued statement for the 'wiped off Israel from the world map'. He reminded in his speeches with evoking Imam Hussein's martyrdom in Karbala that all places on the earth are Karbalas and that "with God's grace, we will soon witness the collapse of the Zionist regime and the destruction of America."[101] His statements against Israel deteriorated Iran's relations with the West and US.

The three important issues – Iran's relations with the United States, Iran's standing in the region, its role within the region, its relationship with Iraq, and its ties with Syria – are all closely intertwined. The Moderates-Reformists Islamists believe that the US presence in the region is uncalled for and the region should be free from the US. In their belief, there should be cooperative efforts among the regional countries aimed at ensuring the region's security and stability. This camp prefers multilateralism at the regional level, which in turn enhanced Iran's standing both regionally and internationally. Deputy Foreign Minister Mohsen Aminzadeh in the Khatami Administration said that Iran has improved its relations with its neighbours, the European Union, the United Nations, and also reduced tensions with US.[102] Iran's Foreign Minister, Mohammad Javad zarif, in the Rouhani Administration has outlined Iran's relations with the outside world that "Iran will expand and deepen its bilateral and multilateral relations through meaningful engagement with a wide range of states and organisation, including international economic institutions. Multilateralism will play a central role in Iran's external relations."[103] The Moderates-Reformists stress on multilateralism and cooperation.

The Conservatives-Radicals Islamists believe that Iran should be an influential and leading country in the region. The region should be free from the US. This camp denounces relationships with the United States. It advocates Iran's engagements with Russia, India, and China, along with a number of other ideologically inclined states.[104] In their view, Iran can play a significant international role within such world environment by maximising its interests and capitalising on its position and its resources. For the Conservatives-Radicals Islamists, Iran's influence and standing in the West Asia in general and in the Persian Gulf in particular, is more than a regional competition with the US. For them, Iran is the centre of Islamic power, and from Iran, Islam grows and thrives throughout the region.

Both camps see as positive the way developments in post-Saddam Iraq have unfolded: the emergence of a political system under the influence of Iraq's Shiite majority and headed by leaders who generally have strong emotion and other attachments with Iran. But both differ on Iran's role in Iraq and how to end the civil war. The Moderates-Reformists favour cooperative approach with the regional countries and foreign powers in resolving Iraq crisis.

The Moderates-Reformists Islamists favour a regionally generated and directed solution to the Iraqi civil war. This camp believes that Saudi Arabia, Egypt, and the European Union should be included in solving the Iraqi civil war. On the other hand, the Conservatives-Radicals Islamists believe that it is Iran's responsibility – by virtue of its influence, diplomatic stature and its role as a bastion of political Islam – to play a leading role in the efforts to end the civil war in Iraq.

Conclusion

The Islamic Republic has been consistently and persistently arguing for independence since the beginning of the Revolution 1979 and even before the revolution religious community, leftists, and liberals criticised the Shah's foreign policy. Iran's outside interaction during the Shah and its effects on polity, economy, society and culture united opposition against the Shah, overthrew monarchy, and produced a new political culture. The Revolution of 1979 completely transformed political culture of Iran and the context of Iran's relations with the foreign countries as well. As domestic politics changed, the new government reversed the Shah's foreign policy orientation and objectives, and ruptured relations with the outside world. Domestic political situation and political dynamics played vital role in shaping the post-Revolution foreign policy.

Iran-Iraq War ceasefire in July 1988, demise of Ayatollah Khomeini in June 1989, economic reconstruction, brought changes in Iran's attitudes towards the outside world. President Hashemi Rafsanjani adopted rapprochement in foreign policy which was continued by Mohammad Khatam. Khatami continued previous government's policies and further expanded Iran's relations with the foreign countries. His moderate policy paid dividend, and Iran's relations with outside world improved. Iran's acceptability regionally and globally increased during Khatami period. As domestic political situation changed in Iran, visible changes ushered in foreign policy arena as had been seen in the Rafsanjani and Khatami periods. Mohammad Khatami's praise to the Western civilisation did not go well in the establishment since clerics struggled against the Shah to free Iran from the US and West. The Conservatives-Radicals Islamists remained suspicious to the US and the West. Khatami's policies provided opportunity to the Conservatives-Radicals Islamists to unite against the moderates. In the June 2005 presidential elections, Mahmoud Ahmedinejad won by defeating the ex-President Hashemi Rafshanjani.

President Ahmedinejad (2005-2013) reversed previous policies and pursued a different diplomacy. He was critical to the West, United States, and Israel, and criticised their attitudes towards Iran. Ahmedinejad pursued pro-active regional policy, and deepened Iran's involvement in the region, thus, strengthened 'strategic depth' in the Arab. His Gulf policy antagonised the regional countries. Ahmedinejad's confrontational foreign policy delved Iran into international isolation, consequently economy was severely affected. The efforts of Rafsanjani and Khatami on foreign policy got a severe jolt, and was actually halted by Ahmedinejad. As domestic political landscape shifts, foreign policy comes under changes that have been seen since the Revolution of 1979.

The June 2009 presidential elections and controversy over its result marked a shift in domestic political equation. The crack appeared within the conservatives groups after this event. The political groups began to organise and reorganise. By 2012, domestic political situation changed Rafsanjani faction and the Moderates-Reformists extended support to Hassan Rouhani during the June 2013 presidential elections. Moreover, a section of the conservatives also extended support to Rouhani. With their supports, Rouhani won presidential elections of the June 2013. President Rouhani has pursued policy of 'constructive engagement' with the outside world. His foreign policy approach is based on moderation, conciliation, and accommodation in order to break Iran's regional and global isolation. Evidently, domestic political dynamics play major role in shaping Iran's foreign policy since composition of support base changes. Policy shifts follow as administrative arrangements change at Tehran. Iran's policy of de-internationalisation has caused a gradual decline in infrastructure, near the absent of foreign investment, political irrelevance, and technological obsolescence.

Endnotes

1   Ayatollah Ali Khamenei belongs to a religious family but not from high-rank religious family. He got education in religious seminaries. He had actively participated in anti-Shah demonstrations and protests. He was sent to prison six times between 1963 and 1978 for his activities against the Shah and in support of Khomeini. He spent about three years in prison and as per his version, he was tortured by SAVAK.

2   The supporters of Furqan carried out the attempt of assassination. Furqan was comprised of the supporters Ali Shariati. It was an Islamic group which opposed clerical rule. The involved persons were arrested and executed. But some have erroneously attributed the assassination attempt to the PMOI. See Morad Veysi, Zendegi Nameh Ayatollah Khamenei" (Biography of Ayatollah

Khamenei), Part 14, *Radio Farda*, available at http://www.radiofarda.com/ autho/hmt; the Persian and English version are not the same.

3   R K Ramazani, *The Foreign Policy of Iran 1500-1941: A Developing Nation in World Affairs* (Charlottesville: University Press of Virginia, 1966), pp. 63-65

4   FBIS-MEA, 13 March 1979, p. R-10

5   Mohandes Mehdi Bazargan, *Enqlab-e Iran dar Dau Harkat* (The Iranian Revolution in Two Phases) (Tehran: Chap-e Sevom, 1362 [1983-84]), pp. 110-111

6   FBIS-MEA, 21 November 1979, p. R-9

7   FBIS-MEA, 20 November 1979, p. R-30

8   FBIS-MEA, 21 December 1979, p. 27.

9   Ibid.

10   R K Ramazani, "Iran: Burying The Hatchet", *Foreign Policy*, no. 60, Fall 1985, p. 62.

11   Anthony Parsons, "Iran And The Western Europe", *Middle East Journal*, vol. 43, no. 2, Spring 1989, p. 225

12   FIBS- MEA, 10 December 1979, p. 29.

13   *Gozaresh-e Seminar* (Tehran), no. 2, 1983/84, p. 36.

14   FBIS- MEA, 14 December 1979, p. 2.

15   FBIS-SA, 31 July 1984, pp. 1-2.

16   FBIS- SA, 7 August 1984, pp. 1-2.

17   Ramazani, n. 10, p. 62

18   FBIS-SA, 30 October 1984, p. 1.

19   FBIS-SA, 4 November 1985, pp. 1-2.

20   Ramajani, n. 10, p. 63

21   Ibid.,

22   Shahrough Akhavi, "Elite Factionalism In The Islamic Republic Of Iran", *Middle East Journal*, vol. 41, no. 2, Spring 1987, p. 201.

23   Anthony H. Cordesman, *The Gulf and the West: Strategic Relations and Military Realities* (London: Westview Press, 1988), p. 310

24   Ibid.,

25   Michael Ledeen, a consultant to the US National Security Council (NSC),

visited Israel on 4-5 May 1985 and talked to senior Israeli officials about Iran. Ledeen met with Israel's Prime Minister Shimon Peres and senior members of Israeli intelligence. Ledeen returned from Israel to US and briefed National Security Advisor Robert McFarlane in mid-May 1985. McFarlane then asked the intelligence community to form a Special National Intelligence Estimate (SNIE) on Iran on 20 May 1985. Secretary of State George Shultz formally objected to Ledeen's activities on 5 June 1985 – and McFarlane advised Shultz on 14 June 1985 that he had instructed him to discourage any arms sale initiative to Iran. However, the NSC proceeded to develop plans for contacts with Iran. These efforts were accelerated when a TWA airline, Flight 847, was hijacked by pro-Iranian groups in Lebanon on 14 June 1985. The issue of US relation with Iran was intensely debated within the US Administration. McFarlane transmitted a draft National Security Decision Directive (NSDD) recommending the option of both arms sales and of intelligence to Secretary of State George Shultz and Secretary of Defence Caspar Weinberger on 17 June 1985. Both secretaries rejected the NSC's proposal in writing. Israeli officials were actively working to encourage US contacts with Iran. David Kimche, Director General of Israel's Foreign Ministry, had visited the White House on 3 July 1985 and asked McFarlane to take up proposal again, stating that his request was on the instructions of Shimon Peres. Another 'private emissary' from Israel visited McFarlane on 13 July 1985. Meanwhile McFarlane visited President Reagan who had just an operation in a hospital during 13-17 July 1985 and talked with him. McFarlane interpreted this conversation as giving him the President's approval of covert contacts with Iran. The hectic contacts between Israel and the US began to establish contacts with Iran. On this issue, President Reagan presided a meeting in the White House on 6 August 1985. The key issue was whether to trade arms for hostages, that President Reagan, Vice President Bush, and the CIA Director William Casey supported the arms initiative, and that Secretaries Shultz and Weinberger opposed it. The meeting was formally practically endorsed arms sales to Iran. The first 100 missiles arrived Iran on 30 August 1985 and remaining 400 arrived on 14 September 1985 through Israel. This arms transfer helped to lead the release of one US hostage Reverend Benjamin Weir on 14 September 1985, but it did not lead to broader release of US hostages that US officials expected. When the US sent arms directly to Iran, one hostage was released. Another shipment of Hawk missiles and Hawk parts went by plane from Israel to Iran in November 1985 but the ship was returned. The flight was authorised by Lt. Colonel Oliver North, of the NSC. Iran repeated this pattern when it released Reverend Lawrence Jenco on 26 July 1986 and David P Jacobsen on 2 November 1986.

26 Two more Southern Air Boeing 707s flew from Texas to Tel Aviv in May 1986, carrying the Hawk parts and TOWs. Then McFarlane, Lt Col. North, George Cave, a CIA official, and Amiran Nir flew to Iran in a plane on 28 May 1986 carrying an initial load of spare parts for the Hawk missiles Iran required to help in protecting its oil facilities. The US officials were supposed

to meet President Ali Khamenei (now the Supreme Leader), Prime Minister Mir Hussein Musavi, and Majlis Speaker Hashemi Rafsanjani, but McFarlane and the rest of his party go few results from their arrival in Tehran. They spent several days waiting in the Tehran Hilton, and talking to low level officials, before being asked to leave. Hashemi Rafsanjni had faced a major problem in dealing with the Americans because Montazeri (declared successor of Ayatollah Khomeini) and chief of staff Mehdi Hashemi – found out about the US visit and strongly opposed it. The Iranian government was as divided about the wisdom of covert dealings with the US as American officials were divided about the merits of dealing with Iran. The US continued its arms sales to Iran despite serious problems in their ties. Iran received TOWs, Hawk parts, and missiles from the US. Iran's relations with US have been still facing challenges as Iranian government is divided over restoring its ties with the US as the US government is divided in dealing with Iran, as was seen in the 1980s. Domestic political dynamics continues to challenge in restoring ties between Iran and the US.

27 Gary Sick, "Trail By Error: Reflections On The Iran-Iraq War", *Middle East Journal*, vol. 43, no. 2, Spring 1989, p. 236

28 Ibid.

29 Ibid.

30 FBIS-SA 9 June 1986, pp. 1-2

31 FBIS-Near East and South Asia (NESA), 4 October 1988, pp. 46-48.

32 FBIS-Near East and South Asia (NESA), 4 October, 1988, pp. 46-48.

33 Mohammad Ali Aminrad, "Hozur Ayatollah Khamenei Dar Roozh-e Moshakbaran Dezful" (Ayatollah Khomenei's Presence at Dezful During the Rains of Rockets), available at http://www.farsi.Khamenei.ir/others-memory?id=19922.

34 See Veysi, "Zindegi Nameh Ayatollah Khamenei".

35 Parsons, n. 11, p. 227

36 Maziar Behrooz, "Factionalism in Iran under Khomeini", *Middle Eastern Studies*, vol. 27, no. 4, October 1991, p. 597.

37 Ibid.,

38 Ibid., p. 598.

39 Ibid., pp. 597-598

40 FBIS-NESA, 11 October, 1988, p. 59

41 FBIS-NESA, 21 October 1988, p. 43.

42 Maryam Panah, *The Islamic Republic and the World: Global Dimensions of the Iranian Revolution* (London: Pluto Press, 2007), p. 118

43 Jahangir Amuzegar, "The Ahmadinejad Era: Preparing For The Apocalypse", *Journal of International Affairs,* vol. 60, no. 2, Spring/Summer 2007, p. 36

44 Bahman Baktiari, "Iran's Conservative Revival", *Current History*, vol. 106, no. 696, January 2007, p. 14

45 Ibid.,

46 Ali M. Ansari, "Iran Under Ahmedinejad: The Politics of Confrontation", *Adelphi Paper 393*, (London: IISS, Routledge, 2007), pp 36-37

47 Karim Sajadpour, "The Nuclear Players", *Journal of International Affairs*, vol. 60, no. 2, Spring/Summer 2007, p. 127

48 Jahangir Amuzegar, "Ahmedinejad's Legacy", *Middle East Policy*, vol. 20, no. 4, Winter 2013, p. 131

49 Mohsen Milani, "Why Tehran Won't Abandon Assad(ism)", *The Washington Quarterly*, vol., 36, no. 4, Fall 2013, p. 83

50 Ibid.,

51 Amuzegar, n. 43, p. 48

52 See excerpts from speech by Iran's Defence Minister General Mostafa Mohammad Najjar in *Resalat*, No. 6091, 22 February 2007

53 www.radiofarda.com, 1 August 2013.

54 Amuzegar, n. 43, p. 35

55 Nader Entessar, "Factional Politics in Post-Khomeini Iran: Domestic and Foreign Policy Implications", *Journal of South Asian and Middle Eastern Studies*, vol. 17, no. 4, Summer 1994, p. 23

56 Ibid.,

57 Ibid., pp. 25-37

58 Ibid., p. 23

59 Ibid., p. 26

60 *Economist*, 31 May, 1997

61 "Khatami Becomes Fifth President", *Iran Times*, 8 August 1997.

62 Trita Parsi, "Europe's Mendacity Doomed Iran Talk to Failure", *Financial Times*, 30 August 2005.

63 *Islamic Republic News Agency (IRNA)*, 7 January 1998.

64 Shabnam J Holliday, *Defining Iran: Politics of Resistance* (Farnham: Ashgate

Publishing Ltd. 2011), p. 111.

65 Mehran Kamrava, "Iranian Natinal-Security Debates: Factionalism and Lost Opportunities", *Middle East Policy*, vol. 16, no. 2, Summer 2007, p. 98.

66 Ibid.,

67 Mohammad Javad Zarif, "What Iran Really Wants: Iranian Foreign Policy in the Rouhani Era", *Foreign Affairs*, vol. 93, no. 3, May/June 2014, p. 51

68 Ibid., p. 57

69 Ibid.,

70 Ibid., p. 58

71 Ibid., p. 59

72 Matteo Lergenzi and Fred H. Lawson, "Iran and Its Neighbours Since 2003: New Dilemmas", *Middle East Policy*, vol. 21, no. 4, Winter 2014

73 W. Andrew Terrill, "Iran's Strategy for Saving Asad", *Middle East Journal*, vol. 69, no. 2, Spring 2015, pp. 229-232

74 Ibid.,

75 Milani, n. 49, p. 84

76 Gawdat Bahgat, "Iran's Relations with Persian Gulf Arab States – Implications for the United States", *Journal of South Asia and Middle Eastern Studies*, vol. 38, no. 2, Winter 2015, pp. 21-22

77 Mohammad Shariati Dahaghan, "Iran Should Not Stand Against the Syrian People", (in Persian), *Iran Diplomacy*, http://www.irdiplomacy.ir/fa/page/12075/html.

78 Mohsen Milani, "Why Tehran Won't Abandon Assad(ism)", *The Washington Quarterly*, vol. 36, no. 4, Fall 2013, p. 84

79 Cited in Jubin Goodarji, "Iran and Syria at the Crossroads: The Fall of the Tehran-Damascus Axis?", Wilson Center, Middle East Programme, Viewpionts series, no 35, August 2013, http://www.wilsoncenter.or/sites/default/files/iran-syria-crossroads-fall-tehran-damascus-axis.pdf

80 Thomas Juneau, "Iran Under Rouhani: Still Alone In The World", *Middle East Policy*, vol. 21, no. 4, Winter 2014, pp. 98-99

81 "Syria is the 35th State", *Asr Iran*, (in Persian), http://www.asriran.com/fa/news/257730

82 Mohsen Milani, "Why Tehran Won't Abandon Assad(ism)", *The Washington Quarterly*, vol. 36, no. 4, Fall 2013, p. 85

83 Shahram Chubin, "Is Iran a Military Threat?", *Survival*, vol. 56, no. 2, April-May 2014, p. 81

84   Ibid.,

85   Ramazani, n. 10, p. 63

86   See Jahangir Amuzegar, "Iran's Economy And The US Sanctions", *Middle East Journal*, vol. 51, no. 2, Spring 1997, pp. 185-199.

87   Data released during Khatami's presidency by the three economic agencies – the Central Bank of Iran, the Management and Plan Organisation, and the Ministry of Finance – but these data are conflicting and contradictory.

88   *Economic Trends*, No. 13, 2005 and *Hamshahri*, 9 April 2005

89   *Economic Trends*, No. 13, 2005 and *Hamshahri*, 9 April 2005

90   Jahangir Amezegar, "Iran's Third Development Plan: An Appraisal", *Middle East Policy*, vol. 12, no. 3, Fall 2005

91   Guy Dinemore, "Iranian Companies Pay the Price for Tehran's Defiance", *Financial Times*, 2 November 2006

92   Gawdat Bahgat, "Iran-Turkey Energy Cooperation: Strategic Implications", Middle East Policy, vol. 21, no. 4, Winter 2014, pp. 126-127

93   www.donya-e-eqtesad.com, 10 December 2006 and www.donya-e-eqtesad.com, 13 January 2007

94   http://emruz.info, 26 December 2006

95   www.radiofarda.com, 7 September 2013

96   Amuzegar, n. 48, p. 131

97   "US Pitting Iranians against Islamic rule", *The Asian Age*, New Delhi, 22 March, 2015, p. 9

98   Amuzegar, n. 86, p. 196

99   Kamrava, n. 65, p. 84

100 Eric Hooglund, "Iranian Views of the Arab-Israeli Conflict", *Journal of Palestine Studies*, vol. 25, no. 1, Autumn 1995, p. 88

101 *Hayat-e*, No. 6072, 28 January 2007.

102 Mohsen Aminzadeh, "Iranian Foreign Policy", http://1384.goooya.com/politics/archieves/2006/04/046129print.php.

103 Mohammad Javad Zarif, "What Iran Really Wants: Iranian Foreign Policy in the Rouhani Era", *Foreign Affairs*, vol. 93, no. 3, May/June 2014, p. 57.

104 Kamrava, n. 65, p. 94

Chapter - 4

Domestic Politics and Security Policy

Domestic situation and political dynamics have been continuously influencing security policy of Iran. The political factions/groups debate over Iran's security policy and issues, and offer policy options. Iran's security policy has been an arena of consistent factional debates and disagreements. There are four main political trends under which each faction operates – the *Rast-e Sunnati* (the Traditional Right), *Rast-e Modern* (the Modern Right), *Chap* (the Left) and *Rast-e Efrati* (the Radical Right). Each political tendency defines Iran's security in its own terms and offers policy options to address it. Each differs in its approach to ensure Iran's security. The political trends are broadly divided into two groups. First and fourth forms the Conservatives-Radicals Islamists coalition while second and third comprises Moderates-Reformists Islamists coalition. Both groups seek to defend, protect, and preserve the Islamic Revolution, the Islamic regime, and territorial integrity, but differ in their approaches. The Supreme Leader, Ayatollah Khamenei, is the final arbiter in pertaining to security policy and issues as Ayatollah Khomeini in the 1980s. Iran's security policy is largely shaped by domestic situation and political dynamics, including external challenges and threats.

All factions profess and adheres an Islamic identity and display commitment to the principles of the constitution of the Islamic Republic. There is unanimity among them over survival of the Islamic regime and its security, but each pursues different approach in ensuring Iran's security. Each pursues a different kind of diplomacy in relation to the country's security. The political factions/groups influence security policy and issues like Iran's forces compositions, forces structures and their deployment, defence industry, weapons acquisition, and nuclear policy. Particularly, Iran's nuclear programme has been an issue of agreement and disagreement among the political factions/groups and intensely debated within Iran. Each successive administration made efforts to modify the previous administration's security policy and succeeded partially/wholly depending on the issues and circumstances.

President Hashemi Rafsanjani (1989-97), President Mohammad Khatami (1997-2005), and President Mahmoud Ahmedinejad (2005-2013), pursued inconsistent security policy as illustrated from the country's behaviour. Each president differed with other, and made efforts to alter partially/wholly Iran's security policy of the previous administration. Security policies and issues have been defined and redefined by the successive regime, administration, and the factions operating at the time. The current President Hassan Rouhani (since August 2013) has been pursuing security policy which seems different from the Ahmedinejad Administration. Particularly, Rouhani's nuclear policy differs with Ahmedinejad policy. Rouhani's nuclear policy and his negotiations with P-5 +1 (US, Britain, France, Russia, China + Germany) have been keenly watched by the Conservatives-Radicals Islamists. Factional approaches remain constant characteristic in defining and redefining security policy despite other factors. Nonetheless, both camps seek to acquire science and technology, peaceful nuclear technology, but they differ in their approaches.

Undoubtedly, there are also other factors which directly and indirectly impinge on country's security. There are variable and invariable factors such as size, topography, geo-location, economic resources, economic development, advanced science and technology, geo-politics, geo-political developments, regional developments, international developments, and international system, which have been consistently and persistently influencing security policy of Iran irrespective of factional approaches on security issues. Iranian leadership has been consistently making efforts to ensure regime security and country's territorial integrity. Iran had faced challenges to its territorial integrity during the eight years war with Iraq (1980-88), and has been consistently facing regime security challenges since the Revolution of 1979. The Islamic Republic has been facing security challenges from the US, including the West since 1979. The US and the West attitudes towards Iran influence Iranian national security thinking and security perception.

Security Perception

The Revolution of 1979 completely transformed Iran, consequently changed security context. Religion coalesced with politics which had far-reaching impact over Iran's security perception. The fusion of religion and politics and its effects appeared in defining and redefining Iran's security following the Revolution. The complex relationship between religion and politics continues to influence security policy and issues. Religion has played a decisive role in building Iran's security perception and national security thinking. Religion was employed in mobilising masses during the Iran-Iraq War to defend and protect the Islamic Revolution, Islamic regime, and territorial integrity. Iran's security was defined and redefined in the 1980s as each State defines its security after the Revolution.

Each State defines its 'security' in terms of territorial integrity, politico-economic autonomy, and socio-cultural vulnerabilities. Security is seen as the ability to secure state survivability, territorial integrity, and ensure political autonomy.[1] The term security has remained a constant discourse in politico-military establishment in pre and post-Revolution Iran. But security definition's connotation has changed in the post-Shah period. The Islamic Republic defines its security in terms of overcoming its social, cultural, politico-military, and territorial vulnerabilities. Moreover, Iran's concept of security includes preserving its ideology upon which the system as a whole is based.

Ideology is one of the basic and most important ingredients in regime's prioritising threats to national security. Contrary to common perceptions, the most serious threats to security are not only military or economic. Ideological threats are serious threats to Iran which Iranian leaders fears most.[2] These are the threats which are posed by the rival cultures that have different sets of values from those of Islam. The Islamic Republic seeks to preserve and protect its Islamic identity and culture.

Iran defines its security in realm of regime survival. Indeed, regime survival is the core issue in the post-Revolution Iran. Several Iranian leaders believe the US is using nuclear issue as a pretext to pursue regime change.[3] Iranian leaders' statements and policies illustrate that regime survival is their core concern.[4] The Islamic Republic seeks to maintain Islam, Islamic traditions and values core to political system of the country, and its preservation priority to the regime. Iranian leadership equates survival of Islam and Islamic traditions with the regime survival.

The Islamic Republic's security concerns are real and legitimate. Iran's security dilemma is tainted by a historical perception of repeated betrayals and letdowns. National experiences have undoubtedly coloured Iranians' perception of other nations' intentions. From the Iranian historical perspective, neither alliance nor neutrality, nor engagement saved Iran from the designs of its enemies. Furthermore, Iran's relations with the Arabs face challenges, and frictions persist. The Conservatives-Radicals Islamists argue about Iran's security in the light of historical experiences and they do not trust the foreigners and the foreign countries. Thus, Iran's security perception is built on historical experiences and current experiences as well.

The Revolution of 1979 did not only transform Iran's polity, but also Iran-US relationship context. Iran's relation with the US defined and redefined in the post-Shah period. The lack of trust between Iran and the US has negatively affected ties between the two countries. The mistrust between Iran and the US has also helped in building Iran's security perception. Iranian leadership does not trust the US due to past experiences and seek the region devoid of the US. The US military presence in the region is a source of concern for Iranian leadership. Iranian leaders have long seen the US military presence in the region as a direct threat to their security.[5] The US has military bases in all neighbouring countries of Iran such as Turkey, Iraq, the UAE, Pakistan, and Afghanistan. The continued US military presence in the region and statements of the US against Iran has strengthened perception among Iranian that it is intended for regime change. Iran also considers Israel as a threat to its security.[6] Israel has issued threats to strike Iran's military installations including nuclear sites.

Israel has linked its security with the West and the US and has signed numerous security and defence pacts with them. The US, the West, and Israel have similar view regarding the Islamic regime in Iran and its nuclear programme.

The United States and the European countries have been consistently and persistently raising questions over legitimacy of the clerical regime in Iran since the Islamic Revolution of 1979. The US has issued threat for military action against Iran and reiterated its intentions at so many occasions. The threat of regime change for the clerical rulers is existential, compelling them to seek the nuclear options. With categorising the US as prime enemy, Iranian defence officials seek to achieve their goals without exceeding political, economic, and human costs they can afford.

President Hashemi Rafsanjani sought to restructure Iran foreign policy orientation and began engagement with the outside world including the US. But the Clinton Administration's 'dual containment' (Iran and Iraq) policy in 1992 discouraged Iran. In the 1990s, Hashemi Rafsanjani and his successor Mohammad Khatami tried to integrate Iran into world system, but was discouraged by the US. Iran was categorised as 'Axis of Evils' in 2002 despite its cooperation with the US during the 2001 war against the Taliban in Afghanistan.[7] Iranian leadership believed that the US has not yet changed its view about Iran despite Tehran's assistance at so many occasions. Their belief became firm again in 2005 when the US Congress passed fund for regime change in Iran. In 2005, the US Congress passed Iran Freedom and Support Act of 2005 which received $ 10 million to fund groups opposed to the Iranian government. President Bush praised the step and called it 'regime change funds'.

The Bush Administration had issued statements of military action against Iran so many times that discouraged the Islamic Republic for engagement with the US. Although President Ahmedinejad wrote letters to President Bush and to the American people for Iran-US relationship, but his efforts remained futile. President Ahmedinejad also sought engagement with the Obama Administration, but Iran's domestic political dynamics and the US posture restrained him for further interaction with the US.

The Obama Administration has continued the previous policy and issued statements of military action against Iran's nuclear installations and facilities. The US-Iran hostility increased during the Ahmedinejad Administration and the US sought to strike against Iran's military establishment. Iran's nuclear programme has become the bone of contention between Iran and the US/West. The tension between Iran and the US/West eased with the election of Hassan Rouhani as president of the Islamic Republic in June 2013. Negotiations on Iran's nuclear programme with the 5+1 (US, Britain, France, Russia, and China + Germany) began and continued till its final outcome. Iran and P-5 + 1 reached an interim agreement in November 2013. But the two sides continued their negotiations for a permanent nuclear agreement, and reached on 14 July 2015. As a result, tensions in Iran-US/West relations eased. Nonetheless, Iran's historical experiences continue to impinge in minds of the Iranian leadership. Particularly, the Conservatives-Radicals Islamists suspect the US/West intention and cite historical experiences.

The oil nationalisation crisis of 1951-53 confirmed Iranians' perception of Western intentions. The treatment of Mohammad Reza Shah (friend and ally of the US for decades) after the Iranian Revolution 1978-79 also confirmed the conviction. Iraq's invasion over Iran in September 1980, Arab and the US support for Saddam Hussein and the silence of all when Iraq used chemical weapons against Iranians confirmed that Iran's interests had to be safeguarded by Iranians and Iranians alone.

Geopolitical Realities

Iran's size, population and resources make it a regional powerful country. Its size is about one-third the size of the US. It is bound by Afghanistan and Pakistan to the east; Azerbaijan, Armenia, Turkmenistan, Kazakhstan and Russia to the north; Iraq and Turkey to the west; and the Persian Gulf and the Gulf of Oman to the south. Iran's Arab neighbours, except Oman, have frictions on several issues. The US military forces in the Persian Gulf, Iraq, Turkey, Central Asia, Pakistan, and Afghanistan surround Iran on all sides. Iraq is in crisis and has been facing serious challenges. As a result of continued crisis in Iraq, Iran has involved herself in the Iraqi affairs to protect its interests.

Instability in the Caucasus, Turkmenistan, Uzbekistan and Tajikistan can spell trouble for Iran. The Islamic Republic is concerned about trouble in these countries. Afghanistan has been continuously facing challenges and continued instability in that country would adversely affect Iran's security. Pakistan has been facing domestic disturbances, internal strife, terrorism, insurgency, and sectarian clashes and can pose security challenges to Iran.

Iran's dispute with the UAE over three islands – Abu Musa, Greater Tunb and Lesser Tunb – are sources of concerns for the Arab countries. The Arab countries continue to extend their supports to the UAE over its dispute with Iran on these three islands. These islands are located closer to Iran's coast or as close to Iran's coast as they are to the UAE shore. An Iranian navy contingent landed on the islands held by Britain a day before the British forces withdrawn from the Persian Gulf in 1971. The presence of the US forces in the Gulf of Oman and the Persian Gulf are source of concerns for the Iran, but the Arab leaders wished to continue the American forces in the region. The root of Arab-Iranian disputes is not simple as many political observers analyse. The Arab-Iran disputes are deep, doctrinal, ideological, and strategic as well. The Arab countries' pronouncements against Iran may convince Iranians that Iran's national security interests coalesce with friendly states and not with those of its Arab neighbours.

Iran-Iraq War and Impact over Iran's National Security Thinking

Iran-Iraq War has had deep impact over Iranian psyche and its national security thinking. Iraq launched simultaneous strikes against all Iranian airfields and military installations within reach of its bombers on 22 September 1980, while it massed armies advanced along a 450-mile front into Iran's Khuzestan province. Iraq placed reasons for attack against Iran, but the real intention was to overthrow the Islamic regime. Iraq's claims of urgent self-defence were less than totally convincing. Observers in the region and elsewhere interpreted these claims as a diplomatic ploy to justify an attempt to overthrow the Islamic regime in Iran that posed a serious threat to Iraqi internal stability.

Iraq believed that Iranian military was so disorganised and demoralised in the wake of a Revolution, that it would no longer be able to sustain a determined military attack; it will change terms of the 1975 Iran-Iraq border agreement to re-establish Iraqi sovereignty over the Shatt al-Arab, as well as regaining Arab control over the Abu Musa, Lesser Tunbs and Greater Tunbs Islands that had Iran occupied in 1971; Iraq's claims over Khuzestan will be realised and Arab population of that territory would welcome Iraq; Ayatollah Khomeini's regime would not survive; and a quick and complete defeat of Iran would shift the balance of power in the Persian Gulf, and Iraq would emerge as a regional power and a leader in Arab politics. Gary Sick observes:

> "Ironically, the results of the Iraqi invasion produced a set of results precisely the opposite of those intended. The attack helped Khomeini to consolidate his control by rallying nationalist sentiments around the revolution, suppressing internal critics, and accelerating efforts to rebuild an effective military machine along Islamic lines. The Arab population of Khuzestan resisted the Iraqi advance. Iraq's military offensive stalled by November 1980 as Iranian resistance stiffened. As Iran began to counterattack effectively, slowly driving Iraqi forces back toward the border, Iraq's great gamble was widely perceived as failure, undermining its regional influence and leaving it far more dependent on the financial and political support of its oil-rich Arab neighbours than ever before."[8]

Indeed, the Iraqi gamble failed and Iraq's dependency on its friends, allies and supporters in the region and beyond grew that undermined its own position in the region and the world.

Iranian Revolution provided impetus to oppositions of the Arab regimes in their respective countries. Imam Khomein and other leaders' appeal to the people of the region and beyond for rise against their unjust rulers had negative effects over Iraq, the Iraqi people, the Arab countries, and beyond. Iraq had faced pressure due to Iran's Revolution and disturbances erupted, that worried the ruling class of Iraq. Saudi Arabia and Bahrain had faced challenges of mass demonstrations and uprisings. The eastern province of Saudi Arabia, Al-Hasa, affected the most since numerically Shia population inhabited in large in the major cities such as Awamyya, Qatif, and Safwa. The Saudi regime faced challenges in containing unrest in this region and other provinces of the country. There also appeared disturbances in other parts of the country, but disturbances in eastern province were severe and alarming for Saudi Arabia and the Saudi regime. Bahrain constitutes majority of Shia population but the ruling family is Sunni minority, and had faced disturbances and mass protests in the aftermath of the Iranian Revolution. The disturbances and demonstrations were severe in Bahrain that worried its rulers. Even in February and March 2011, Bahrain faced large mass demonstrations and protests that caused Saudi Arabia's military intervention in that country to restore normalcy. The Saudi forces entered Bahrain in March 2011 to protect ruler of Sunni minority and restore normalcy in the country.

Iraq's war over Iran intended to dissolve the Islamic regime since Iranian Revolution had become a source of inspirations to the people of the region and beyond. But Iraq's war against Iran could not yield expected result and the Islamic regime did not only survive, but also consolidated and strengthened during the eight years of war. Ayatollah Khomeini and other leaders vowed to the complete defeat of Iraq but changed their views due to growing circumstances at home and beyond and accepted ceasefire in July 1988. Iranian leadership saw no sign of complete defeat to Iraq, and situation was also changing at home and beyond.

Ayatollah Khomeini's announcement of Iran-Iraq War ceasefire startled not only the world, but also the Iranian. As Iran-Iraq War dragged on, resources exhausted, and sign of victory was not visible. The shortage of resources, fatigue with war, and deteriorating economy, were responsible factors for acceptance of ceasefire. Ayatollah Khomeini accepted the proposal of ceasefire in 1988. "Iran's decision to accept the cease-fire and to commit itself seriously to the peace process reflects an acute interplay between its battle-fields setbacks and its deteriorating socioeconomic conditions."[9] Until February 1987, Iranian leadership had repeatedly promised a 'final victory', and once even specified a decisive victory by 21 March 1987, the Iranian New Year. Iran's Karbala-5 offensive threatened Basra and sent shockwaves throughout the Gulf and to the US/West. Despite its failure or because of the massive loss of lives of the Revolutionary Guards, Tehran realised that the war could not be won. Hashemi Rafsanjani candidly said: "To tell the truth, we cannot see a bright horizon now, so far as ending the war in its present form is concerned. . . ."[10] In July 1987, for the first time, Iran did not reject a UN Security Council resolution outright, although Resolution 598 was more sensitive to Iran's positions that the previous ones. The Islamic Republic had quietly opted for a diplomatic solution to the war, probably after the effects of the disastrous Karbala-offensive that sank into the consciousness of Iranian leadership. Subsequent battlefields setbacks at Faw Peninsula, the Majnun islands, and Shalamjah beginning in April 1988, compelled Iranian leadership for a diplomatic solution, although UN Secretary General Javier Perez de Cuellar had involved into discussions long before these setbacks.

Iran had been facing economic crisis in 1986 and 1987. The intense war in 1986-87, dramatic drop in oil revenues due to unprecedented fall in oil prices in 1986, and an equally unprecedented increase in Iraq's capability for disrupting Iranian oil exports, caused widespread economic hardship in Iran. The issue of economic reform also caused economic hardship. Both camps, the Conservatives-Radicals and the Moderates, stuck to their positions on economic policy. Ayatollah Khomeini tried to break the long-standing logjam on measures for social justice and economic betterment caused by the veto of government reform bills by the conservative members of the Council of Guardians. He created a 13-member review council to oversee the decisions of the Council of Guardians in "the interest of the Islamic country".[11] Ayatollah Khomeini accepted the ceasefire on 18 July 1988 in a war that he could not win, he opted it for the survival of his regime and the Islamic Revolution. The Iran-Iraq War had deep impact over Iranian psyche and convinced the Iranian leadership to develop a credible deterrent.

Historical experiences, Iran-Iraq War, and the attitudes of the world major powers towards war forced Iranian leadership to develop a credible deterrent. Iranian leadership believed that the country's security must be based on deterrence. A conventional force based on the domestic resources, technology and industrial capacity, could not overcome security challenges. A credible nuclear deterrence with a reliable missile requires Iran. A nuclear deterrence, would afford Iran not supremacy of power in the region, but a balance of power that it could not otherwise have.[12] This thinking gained ground in the 1980s, but Imam Khomeini was against development of nuclear arsenals. However, after demise of Ayatollah Khomeini, Iranian leadership made efforts to acquire deterrent capability and pursued nuclear programme.

Strategic Culture

What is strategic culture? The concept of strategic culture made debut in the 1970s. Jack Snyder, RAND analyst, explained strategic culture in 1977 with an analysis of the Soviet limited nuclear warfare doctrine. The concept, first proposed in a RAND Report called *The Soviet Strategic Culture: Implications for Limited Nuclear Operations* (September 1977) that defined strategic culture as "the sum total of ideas, conditioned emotional responses and patterns of habitual behaviour that members of a national strategic community have acquired through instruction or imitation."[13] Snyder argues in the RAND Report that 'Soviet strategic thought and behaviour' originated from 'a distinctively Soviet strategic culture'.

Colin S. Gray's article "National Style in Strategy: The American Example" came out in the *International Security* (1981), explained American strategic culture with analysis of American modes of thought and action with respect to force, derives from perception of the national historical experience, aspiration for self-characterisation, geography, political philosophy, and civil culture.[14] He envisages that the idea of an American national style is derived from the idea of American strategic culture, and makes suggestions that there is a distinct American way in strategic matters. He points out, first, an American strategic culture flows from geopolitical, historical, economic and other unique influences; second, American strategic culture provides the milieu within which strategic ideas and defence policy decisions are debated and decided; third, an understanding of American strategic culture can help explain why American policy makers have made decisions they have.[15] Moreover, if the past and present can be explained, it will be possible to use the concept of strategic culture to predict decisions in future. The concept of strategic culture defines as that set of shared beliefs, assumptions, and modes of behaviour, derived from common experiences and accepted narratives (both oral and written) that shape collective identity and relationships to other groups, and which determine appropriate ends and means for achieving security objectives.[16] No doubt, every state has its own history, historical experiences, belief, culture, value, social, political and economic system, resources and capability which influence thinking of the people of that country.

Nonetheless, there is no consensus among the scholars on how to define the concept of strategic culture. Scholars agree that strategic culture is the product of a combination factors, primarily state ideology, culture, belief, historical experiences, geography, economic resources, economic development, level of technology, and international order.[17] Some political analysts have argued the components of Iranian strategic culture such as ideology, culture, historical experiences, geography, economic resources, level of economic development, world system, and its distinct Persian character can better explain Iranian behaviour. There is disagreement among the scholars about the extent of Islam's influence over policy-making in Iran. For them, religion is one of the variables but not the whole. It will be oversimplification here to deny the role of Islam in Iran's behaviour. Islam an ideology functions in influencing strategic culture of Iran. In the post-Revolution, Islam has exercised a disproportionate influence relative to other factors in shaping state policy with respect to employment of forces and Iran's behaviour.

As an ideology, Shiite Islam has deeply influenced strategic culture of Iran. It has deep influence on Iran's world view and action plan. The Iranian leadership first sketches picture of the world in which it has to operate, categorises who are its friends and enemies, and where it interests lies. In this process, it advises how to relate to the outside world, what its foreign policy goals should be, and how to behave with the outside world. The action plan advises Iran how to run the country, how to develop its armed forces and when, where, and how to employ the armed forces to achieve national objectives. The fusion of religion with politics reflects that Islam has deeply affected Iranian strategic culture. Iran's strategic culture is also shaped, and deeply affected by other factors.

Security Strategy

In 1979, Iran's revisionist foreign policy had far-reaching implications on its defence posture. Iran's foreign policy soured its relations with regional and foreign countries. Iran lost its friends and allies with whom had shared relations. As a result, Iran could no longer rely on alliance with major powers to ensure its security. Iran did not have any ally among major powers and powerful regional friends, and it was forced to rely on its own resources to ensure internal and external security. In order to ensure its security, several measures were taken: creating an ideological army, mobilisation of masses for defence of the country, developing defence industries, weapons acquisition, and forging close relations with Islamic movements in the West Asia.

The Islamic Republic formed the IRGC, *Basej,* and other institutions to defend, protect, and preserve the Islamic Revolution and the Islamic regime. It stressed on self-reliance in military industrialisation, though it knew constrains. Iran realised that it could not achieve military self-sufficiency without foreign assistance. It got weapons and military technology wherever it could, and imported arms which it could not make itself. The self-sufficiency approach in defence was reinforced by the American-hostage crisis at Tehran (November 1979 - January 1981), Iraq's invasion over Iran, and the US/West sanctions after the Revolution. Iran also forged close ties with the Islamic movements in the region and used as proxies to put pressure on its enemies.

Iran took measures to bolster its defence capability. It started to develop defence industries that the country could achieve self-sufficiency in design, manufacture, maintenance, and operation of weaponry. It believed that self-sufficiency was essential if Iran was not to fall under foreign domination. They viewed that any reliance on outsiders for its defence requirements would make Iran susceptible to external pressures, compromise seriously its ability to defend the Muslim homeland, and thereby reduce the deterrence capability of the armed forces.[18] Thus, self-sufficiency became cornerstone of security strategy in the post-Shah period.

The Shah's military industrialisation programme was characterised by heavy dependence on the US, the West, and Western arms industries in all fields. Iran relied on the West and US for the transfer of technology and the training of the Iranian engineers, technicians, and managers to operate the defence plants and industries and they were under contract to build. It was also heavily dependent on the US/West firms for conducting the research and development required to modify the US and the Western equipment to suit Iran's particular requirements and conditions. Iran also relied extensively on foreign engineers and technicians, and instructors from a number of countries to run its military industrial complex. Thus, Iran was heavily dependent on the US and the West for its arms requirements. As the Revolution 1979 ruptured relations with the US and the West, weapons supply from the US and the West dried up.

Iran had faced shortages of arms due to supplier nations' interruption or embargoes during its war with Iraq. Particularly after 1986, when 'Operation Staunch' was more rigorously implemented by the US, cutting off Iranian access to spare parts and new weapons, Iran had difficulties in sustaining its war efforts. As the war continued, cannibalising parts and improvising repairing and maintenance became difficult, and replacements became more costly. As a result, in the post-war Iran, self-reliance became the watch word, in practice a mixture of domestic production, diversification of sources of supply and stockpiling of arms and spare parts sufficient to carry on in the events of major supply interruptions.[19] In the post-war period, the Islamic Republic concentrated its efforts to make the country self-sufficient in defence matter.

Iranian leadership was forced to rethink its defence industrialisation strategy. Iran's hostility to the US/West, and the latter's perception of Iran as disruptive force in West Asia, it was not possible to rely on the US/West for arms. It initiated plans that emphasised on effective mobilisation of domestic resources for military self-sufficiency. Moreover, Iran looked new partners abroad, which could provide Iran with military know-how, production technology, arms, and other defence related items and technology that it could not yet produce.

In the early 1980s, Iran entered into contracts with countries like China and North Korea. Iran did not only buy weapons from China and North Korea but also received technology and got assistance in construction of military industrial complexes.[20] China first sold Iran anti-ship cruise missile (ASCMs) and then set up factories that produced various types of

ASCMs inside the country. North Korea transferred technology required to produce Scud-B ballistic missiles to Iran.[21] Moreover, Iran obtained arms and ammunitions from countries such as Russia and Ukraine.

In the 1990s, situation changed within Iran and in the region. Iran had benefited from Iraq's defeat in the Gulf War 1991-92, West's subsequent containment of Baghdad, and its own geographical position in the Gulf. Iran held no illusions about its security in the rough neighbourhood of southwest Asia. As years passed, Iranian leaders faced challenges from Iraq, instability in Central Asia, Lebanon-Israel tension, and the Taliban's ascendency to power in Afghanistan. In these circumstances, Iranian leaders began to move security policy toward detente and deterrence to make the strategic context more favourable to develop Iran's military power.

Iran also made efforts to enhance research and development capacity of the armed forces. The Defence Industries Organisation, which is the primary body responsible for arms production, opened new research institutes within the Ministry of Defence, and signed various contracts with Iranian universities to undertake research on defence related issues. Moreover, Iranian universities started new programmes that trained students in areas that had direct military applications like robotics and aerospace engineering. As a result, a large number of scientists and engineers were produced by the universities related to defence issues.

Iran also began a programme of systematic and extensive reverse engineering of components, weapon systems, and entire platform to alleviate the shortage of spare parts for its US and West made weapons. Reverse engineering made a significant contribution to replenish Iran's arms and maintain weapons systems in working conditions. However, Iran still has to buy some sophisticated arsenals and components on the black market or through front companies. Now, Iran's defence industries have reached to a stage that they can design and produce many of their own weapon systems. They include radar systems, unmanned aerial vehicles, surface-to-surface ballistic missiles, surface-to-air missile systems, frigates and fast patrol boats.[22] Iran mobilised its domestic resources to produce own arms, and partially succeeded.

As a part of security strategy, Iran floated the idea of regional security arrangements and made efforts to realise it. A multi-layered security arrangement required to defend the region and the regional states. In Iran's belief, a regional security arrangement should be multi-layered and multi-dimensional, which will allow configuration of complete balance of power among smaller states, between smaller states as a group and large ones, and finally among groups of small and medium sized states collectively on the one hand, and much larger dominant ones on the other. It will be regional, flexible, and self-adjusting.

Iranian officials changed their security strategy and started to outline defensive strategies between 2001 and 2003 that stressed ideological dimension of Iran's security perceptions. The Revolutionary Guard's Command College in 2001 published a book that included several military doctrines. These doctrines stressed on faith, devotion, mobilisation, and the use of pro-revolutionary organisations beyond Iran's borders.[23] By 2005, Iran became confident as saw its security strengthened with the overthrow of Saddam and the US forces were increasingly involved and bogged down in Iraq.[24] Iran's officials were concerned about the US forces around Iran, but they were pleased to see that the US was entrapped in the region.

In the post-Saddam Iraq, Iran continues to cultivate Iraq and has signed several agreements including cultural, social, economic, political, strategic, defence, and security. Iran seeks to maintain friendly relations with Iraq and a pro-Iran government in Baghdad to alleviate security concerns at its western border since Iran had been continuously facing security challenges at its western border during the Saddam period. In the post-Saddam period, Iran's involvement in Iraq grew. Iran grabbed opportunity and increased its influence and presence in Iraq by cultivating various *Shia* groups and factions. Iran-Iraq ties further expanded and deepened during the Ahmedinejad presidency and Iran's involvement in Iraq grew.

Iran's President Rouhani vowed in June 2014 that Iran would extend every possible support to Iraq in tackling crisis. Iran is physically, militarily and materially involved in defending Iraq's territorial integrity and its forces are fighting side by side with Iraqi forces against Sunni insurgents who have occupied several strategic points and provinces including Mosul and Anbar. Colonel Shoja'at Almdari Mourjani was killed during fighting in the city of Samarra, north of Baghdad on 5 July 2014.[25] Mourjani's death came after Iran's declaration that it would provide its western neighbour with whatever needs to counter the Sunni insurgents who are lying siege to the Shia-led government of Prime Minister Nuri al-Maliki.[26] Iran has been continuously providing every possible help to Iraq.

Iran's involvement in Iraq has grown and deepened as Iraqi forces failed to protect its territory from the Sunni insurgents and the Islamic State (IS) designs. Iraqi forces and militia fighters captured part of Tikrit's northern Qadisiya district on 11 March 2015. More than 20000 Iraqi troops and Iranian-backed *Shia* militia known as *Hashid Shaabi* launched an offensive in the early March 2015 and seized part of Qadisiya district on 11 March 2015.[27] Reportedly, Iran's Islamic Revolutionary Guard Corps personnel are involved in this conflict and fighting side by side with Iraqi forces against the *Sunni* insurgents and the IS to regain territory.[28] Iran has sent military personnel to help Iraq and Iraqi forces and they are also providing training and advice to the Iraqi forces. Thus, the Islamic Republic has involved herself financially, materially, and physically in Iraq in order to protect its strategic interests.

Military Doctrine

With overthrow of the Shah in 1979, Iran departed from the US and the West oriented security alliances. Iran's departure from the Western and American security alliances caused loss of allies and friends. Subsequently the Islamic regime faced security challenges from the US and the West. A new political culture emerged following the Revolution that completely changed security discourse and strategy. Iran adopted military doctrine and security strategy to defend and protect the country's territorial integrity, the Islamic regime, and the Islamic Revolution.

Without allies, the Islamic Republic required doctrine and resources to defend the country. The Islamic regime developed military forces and resources to ensure the Islamic Republic's security. Military doctrine was evolved to meet Iran's immediate and future challenges. Ayatollah

Khomeini, the founder of the Islamic Republic, laid the foundation of military doctrine, ensured that Islam would be a cornerstone for Iran's conception of war and military doctrine.[29] Iran formally adopted military doctrine in the early 1990s though its evolution began in the 1980s. The military doctrine was adopted and codified in 1992 in the regulations of the Iranian Armed Forces, which remain an essential starting point to understand Iran's defence doctrine.[30] The regulations were an attempt to build on wartime experiences, military ongoing missions, and evaluation of threats from actual and potential enemies.

Military doctrine stressed on self-reliance, conventional weapons, unconventional weapons, ballistic missile based deterrence, nuclear options, unconventional operations, Iran's strategic depth, and popular mobilisation of warfare. The main factors which convinced Iran to develop a post-war doctrine included the losses of men and weapons during the Iran-Iraq War 1980-88 and the success of US efforts to restrict weapons sales to Iran. When the basic principles of Iranian military and strategy doctrine were formalised in 1992, Iran lacked weapons, technology and basic resources, but had to rely on geography, domestic resources, manpower resources, nationalistic and revolutionary fervour.

Iran's military posture is largely defensive.[31] The Iranian forces are configured for defence, and repeatedly declared, is defensive. Iran defines success in terms of thwarting the enemy's goals. The outlined principles in the regulations are statements of national security policy and they linked to defensive - Iran's defensive goals of protecting and preserving national independence, territorial integrity, *Velayat-e Faqih*, the Islamic regime, the Islamic Revolution, national interests, regional interests, and other Muslim and oppressed nations. The principles put emphasis on Islam as a basic concept for organising and equipping the Armed Forces. They also stress on loyalty to the *Valayat-e Faqih*, seek self-sufficiency in defence, and to defend, and deter. It stresses to punish aggressor against Iran and oppressed nations – as the prime goal of the Armed Forces. Military doctrine puts emphasis on the loyalty to the concept of *Velayat-e Faqih* that strengthens the position of the Supreme Leader. The regulations stress on maintenance of Islamic values, culture, and standards. In the Islamic Republic's military doctrine, spirituality and military discipline is linked.

Military doctrine focuses on challenges, threats and opportunities, the character of the war, the missions and goals of the Armed Forces and the present and future forces structure needed to provide resources to complete the means-ends chain of national security policy. Iran's military capabilities are limited; therefore, it has pursued a deterrence-based doctrine that stresses an adversary's risks and costs. In nutshell, Iran's concept of war seeks to avoid conventional military conflict, especially with the United States, and rely on irregular warfare and asymmetric warfare.

The doctrine also tries to bring coherency in plans for arms acquisitions and unit formations. It includes how to proceed for arms acquisitions and unit structures. Military doctrine has also future plans regarding forces structures, arms acquisitions, and wars. The Islamic Republic has developed its military and enhanced its military capability despite the West and US challenges. Iran's defence capability has increased tremendously and is relatively militarily strongest among the regional countries. It has increased its area of influence in the region and pursued pro-active regional policy.

When Iraq used chemical weapons against Iranian forces on the war fronts during Ira-Iraq War, Ayatollah Khomeini forbade the Iranian military for producing and using poison gas against Iraq on the grounds that these weapons are inhumane. Ayatollah Khomeini did not allow production of poisonous gas but after Iran-Iraq War appeared that Iran had produced and stockpiled chemical agents, though it had not used against Iraqi troops.[32] Iran's current Supreme Leader, Ayatollah Khamenei, has rejected any role for nuclear weapons in Iran's defence doctrine on the same ground, as Ayatollah Khomeini.

Iran's leadership believes that strong faith will lead to victory. In Iranian leadership beliefs, the fate of the battle is decided not by the number of men, nor by the quantity and quality of weapons that it bears but by the strength of faith in the soldiers. The strong faith increases certainty for victory. Faith can compensate for inferiority in numbers and weaponry. It means that in war the size of the armed forces, the quality and quantity of weapons, and its strategy and tactics are insignificant. Nonetheless, the size of the armed forces, the quality and quantity of arms, and strategy and tactics are important, but the faith plays the decisive role in the war. In Ayatollah Khomeini's view, blood is victorious over the swords.[33] Iranian leaders gained experience during the Iran-Iraq War that faith was definitely important in the war, so were strategy, tactics, training, discipline, and the quality and quantity of weapons. They talk in historical context. Actually, it has deep roots in the history of Shiite Islam. Iranian leaders always refer to the historic Battle of Karbala. In the Islamic history, the Battle of Karbala carries high significance since it was fought between Hussein Ibn Ali, the third Shiite Imam, and Yazid, the second Umayyad Caliph in 680 AD.[34] Yazid had many thousands forces whereas Imam Hussein had to rely on less than hundred. Imam Hussein and his followers and forces fought against adversary despite certainty of defeat, they defeated and perished in the Battle of Karbala. The Shiite Islam considers Imam Hussein and his followers as victorious since they carried out their responsibility to defend Islam from Umayyads.

At the strategic level, ideology also affected Iran's alliances during Iran-Iraq-War. Ideology transformed Iran's foreign policy which sought to remake the world. The Islamic Republic had been seen as a threat by those, who wanted status-quo. The regional countries wished to maintain status-quo which was supported by the West and the US. Iran sought to alter pattern of interactions with the US and the West because conflict of their interests. The United States and the West sought to maintain status quo in the region to serve their strategic interests.

Islam has not only transformed Iran's polity, society, and foreign policy, but also security policy and battle strategy. The impact of Islam is most felt at the level of national security objectives, military strategy, and to a lesser extent at the level of operational strategy. Islam's impact is more visible with respect to broad issues pertaining to the use of force than the minor matters of battlefield tactics. It also influences battlefield strategy. Tactical issues of the battlefield are entirely shaped by non-ideological factors and strategic culture.

The other doctrine as 'deterrence by denial' involves ground forces. If Iran will be invaded, it would take advantage of its strategic depth by fighting a people's war with its lightly armed and trained, and committed

Basej forces. Iran may use the *Hizb-e Allah* and the Islamic Amal of Lebanon to raise costs of its adversary. Thus, strategy may enhance cost of adversary and opponents' resources will be diverted towards defence to its interests in other part of the region and the world.

Deterrence remained cornerstone of Iran's security strategy. Iran's military capability is limited. It has pursued a deterrence-based doctrine that stresses raising costs and risks of the adversary. Iran seeks to reduce its costs and risks by maximising its passive defences and taking advantages of its strategic depth and manpower mobilisation capabilities, and would raise costs to its opponents through attrition and unconventional warfare anywhere in the world.

Iranian leadership believe that Islam does not sanction offensive military operations. Whether Iran will use its military capabilities in an offensive way in the future, is uncertain. Iranian military strategy is defensive, but it does not mean that in the event of war the Iranian military would stop at the borders after driving out the enemy from its territory. As the Iran-Iraq War illustrates, once the invading Iraqi forces had been pushed out of the country after two years of fighting, Iran pursued the enemy into its territory and fought war for six more years. Even Iran occupied the Faw Peninsula of Iraq in February 1986.

After the US invasion over Afghanistan and Iraq, Iran brought changes in its military doctrine and introduced asymmetric warfare. Iran changed its military doctrine to favour asymmetric warfare, and stressed on importance of human resources over military equipment.[35] Strategically, Iran has changed its tactics of war in order to ensure its security. Basically, Iran's military doctrine witnessed a little revision like asymmetric warfare in the early 2000s.

Mohammad Khatami sought to improve Iran's relations with the neighbours and the European countries which had been pursued by his predecessor, Hashemi Rafsanjani. President Khatami pursued policy of detente and engagement with the neighbours and the European countries. This policy was adopted to secure balance of power in the region militarily and diplomatically. Iran's Defence Minister, Ali Shamkhani under President Khatami said in 2000 that Iran's defence industry, structural organisation, defence policy, military doctrine, and training and education "are dependent on our policy of detente."[36] Mohammad Khatami's approach welcomed the regional countries, and Tehran-Riyadh relations steadily began to improve. Iran's relations with the Arab countries deteriorated during Ahmedinejad period due to his assertive regional and defence policy.

Mahmoud Ahmedinejad's pro-active regional policy and nuclear policy deteriorated Iran's relations with the Arab countries, the US, and European countries. Indeed, deterioration in Iran's relations with the Arab countries, the US and European countries began by the end of the Khatami period. But tensions in their relations rose during the Ahmedinejad period. With the election of Hassan Rouhani as president in the June 2013 presidential elections, Iran's relations with the Arab countries, the US, and the European countries eased. His policy of 'constructive engagement' with the outside world appears defensive in respect with defence and strategy.

Formation of Ideological Forces

Iran's strategic culture advocated maximum reliance on domestic resources for the defence of Islamic Revolution and the Islamic regime from external threats in the absence of external supports since Iran's relations had soured with the outside world. Iran could no longer rely on alliance with major powers to ensure its security. This led to initiate several measures. The Islamic Republic formed the IRGC, *Basej* and other institutions to defend, protect, and preserve the Islamic regime and the Islamic Revolution. The religious masses which had been instrumental in overthrowing monarchy were mobilised to defend, protect, and preserve the Islamic Revolution. In this way, the *Basej* was born. The IRGC was formed in May 1979 to defend and protect the Islamic Revolution too.

Ayatollah Khomeini immediately established an Islamic army to protect the Islamic state. In the early May 1979, the regime issued a decree that called for the establishment of the Islamic Revolutionary Guard Corps (IRGC). This was to be an army whose personnel were selected from among the most devout Muslims. The IRGC comprised former members of the Islamic urban guerrilla forces fought against the Shah's regime, Islamist opponents of the Shah who had received military training in the

Palestinian Liberation Organisation's camps in Lebanon, and the religious members of the Shah's army. In order to expand its ranks, the IRGC started recruitment from amongst the most pious and devout Muslims and active supporters of the Revolution. The regime also made efforts to convert the Shah's military forces, often referred to as the regular military, to a force that side by side with the IRGC could play a part in defending the state from the external threats. This mission was achieved gradually through purging the Shah's military, ideological indoctrination, and recruitment of the faithful. The regime purged military by removing and hanging personnel.

Ayatollah Khomeini ordered on 26 November 1979 for the formation of *Basej-e Mustazafin* (the Mobilisation of the Deprived). The *Basej* was founded to mobilise, train, arm, and organise all adult Iranian men and women to defend and protect the Islamic Republic. Basically, the formation of the *Basej* was in response to perceived domestic and external threats. The rebellions in some parts of the country (Kurdistan, Khuzestan, and Torkaman Sahra), uncertainty about the ability of the regular military to tackle these threats, and after beginning of the American-hostages crisis on 4 November 1979, the perceived threat from the US, all acted as a catalyst in formation of the *Basej*. In the beginning, the *Basej* was an independent organisation, but in the late 1980 it was subordinated to the IRGC.[37] The *Basej* and the IRGC constitute as the Islamic army to defend the Islamic Republic and the Islamic Revolution.

The IRGC and *Basej* have special features and they are primarily motivated by ideology. These two organisations fought during the Iran-Iraq War 1980-88 to defend Iranian territory, the Islamic regime, and the Islamic Revolution. They have fought to protect not only territorial integrity of the country, but also the Islamic regime, and the Islamic Revolution. Their role in Iran gradually expanded and obtained government contracts in developing infrastructures, and economy.

Nuclear Policy and Factional Approaches

Mohammad Reza Shah initiated nuclear development programme to acquire nuclear weapons. With overthrow of the Shah in 1979, Ayatollah Khomeini led Iran and declared that nuclear weapons were forbidden in

Islam, and halted programme.[38] Ayatollah Khomeini forbade use of nuclear weapons. He reiterated this position on various occasions, and it remained official line till his death. His successor, Ayatollah Khamenei has argued the same, and declared that nuclear arsenals in Islam are forbidden.

In the post-Shah period, the *Velayat-e Faqih* had shaped the public debate on nuclear weapons with Islam, and its stance on the development and use of nuclear weapons. There is no consensus among the *ulema* on the permissibility of development and use of nuclear weapons within Islam. However, some experts have debated over this complex issue. This study confines to explain only Iran since enlargement of the discourse will digress the study.

The debate over nuclear policy remained confined to the ruling elites in Tehran before Ahmedinejad elected as president. Ahmedinejad's election heralded assertion in Iran's nuclear policy, and opened debate over it.[39] President Ahmedinejad successfully pulled the debate on Iran's nuclear policy out of discrete purview of policy elites into the public domain.[40] In doing so, Ahmedinejad framed the nuclear issue as one of "national independence that would stymie foreign powers seeking to deprive Iran of its rightful place – as a major international and technological power."[41] As a result, political factions/groups have publicly debated nuclear policy and aired their views. Numerous literatures reflect that Iran's ruling elites and general public are unanimous that Iran should have a "full nuclear fuel cycle."[42] There exists a national consensus in Iran over its nuclear programme which is widely shared among all classes and social groups that Iran should have nuclear technology, if not nuclear weapons, and no foreign power has the right to deny Iran access to nuclear technology.[43] Various studies point out that elites use a number of arguments to garner public support for their positions regarding any issue including nuclear. These points and arguments may be based on security considerations, or appeals to national pride, religion, or other values.[44] The elites use all possible forums to garner public supports on important issues which they consider.

Undoubtedly, Iran's leaders are interested in nuclear technology in general and nuclear deterrence in particular. Particularly, on nuclear technology, most Iranians are supportive of their leaders' policies.[45] Iran also takes nuclear programme as prestige issue and seeks to acquire. Iranians tend to support the nuclear programme as a matter of national pride.[46] Iranians see acquisition of nuclear technology/weapon as a matter of international prestige – the recognition of Iran's high status among other regional actors.[47] Developments illustrate that Iranian public opinion matters in influencing the decisions of the administration. Iran regularly holds elections at federal and sub-national levels, and reflects the significance of popular opinions on domestic and foreign policy issues. These elections demonstrate public's preferences. Political factions/groups offer their policy preferences during elections, and people prefer one over other.

The current Supreme Leader, Ayatollah Khamenei, has rejected any role for nuclear weapons in Iran's defence doctrine on the same grounds as Ayatollah Khomeini did. He has issued a *fatwa* banning the production and deployment of nuclear arms.[48] The *fatwa* was also published by Iran's *Mehr News Agency* in 2005 which reads as "The Leader of the Islamic Republic of Iran, Ayatllah Ali Khamenei, has issued the *fatwa* that the production, stockpiling, and use of nuclear weapons are forbidden under Islam and the Islamic Republic of Iran shall never acquire these weapons."[49] Ayatollah Khamenei has repeatedly stated this position at several public forums in Iran. In May 2012, Ayatollah Khamenei stated: "From an ideological and juridical point of perspective, we consider developing nuclear weapons unlawful. We consider using such weapons a big sin. We also believe that keeping such weapons is futile and dangerous and we will never go after them."[50] He has been consistently denying the role of nuclear weapons in Iran' defence doctrine, as his predecessor denied.

It is noteworthy that Ayatollah Khomeini and Ayatollah Khamenei, Iran's Supreme Leaders and the most important voices on religion, have publicly stated that Islam forbids the development of nuclear weapons and its use. These pronouncements would help in shaping the public opinion on nuclear policy of Iran. The studies have shown that religious pronouncements and arguments about security policy and other political issues get appeal in societies. In fact, in Islamic societies where Islam has deep roots and where society takes its religion very seriously, affect public opinion, such as Iran. Ayatollah Khamenei is Supreme Leader, he is a legitimate source of opinion on the matter of nuclear weapons and his words on matters of Islam and security issues would carry substantial weight, since he follows the same line as the late Ayatollah Khomeini. Nonetheless, Iranian society is divided on nuclear policy despite pronouncements of Ayatollah Khomeini and Ayatollah Khamenei.

Political factions/groups are divided on nuclear policy as public opinion is divided. All Iranian may not agree with Ayatollah Khamenei's view on Islam regarding nuclear issue. The Conservatives-Radical Islamists advocates that nuclear weapon is permissible in Islam. However, Islam's stance on nuclear weapons will not be only driving factor for development of nuclear arsenals. This section offers other considerations for development of nuclear weapons such as perceived threats that Iran faces from other countries. The Conservatives-Radical Islamists views the world as an inherently hostile place and "their country must develop a strong deterrent capability in the form of nuclear weapons."[51] Thus, other considerations would provide ground for development of nuclear weapons and its use.

The Programme on International Policy Attitudes (PIPA) and Search for Common Ground (SCG) conducted survey of 710 respondents on Iran's nuclear weapons from 13 January 2008 to 9 February 2008. The PIPA/ SCG 2008 survey reveals Iranian public opinion on nuclear issue. Those who believe that the US will attack on Iran, are inclined to acquire nuclear weapons; the perceived threat posed to Iran by the US having military bases in the West Asia; and those who see the US military bases as a major threat want Iran for possessing nuclear weapons.[52] In Iran's belief, the US poses serious security threat to the Islamic Revolution and the Islamic regime. Moreover, those who want to increase influence and power of Iran support development of nuclear weapons. Iranian who believe that there are a number of secret nuclear programmes in the world they seek Iran to acquire nuclear weapons. The survey reveals that women, young Iranians, Tehran residents, and less educated individuals want Iran to move towards developing nuclear weapons.[53] The debate on issue of Iran's nuclear weapons programme continues within Iran and beyond. Whether Islam allows nuclear weapons or not, but security consideration may force Iran to acquire nuclear weapons.

Iranian Leadership frequently points out that the US is making false allegations against Iran for its peaceful civil nuclear programme, and the US simultaneously offers a substantial military, economic, and political support to nuclear-armed states such as Israel, India, and Pakistan who are not signatories to the NPT and do not allow international inspections of their nuclear facilities.[54] This apparent double standard raises concerns among Iranian politicians that the true aim of the US is to curb Iranian power and to foster internal domestic dissent that will ultimately lead to overthrow of the current regime in Iran.[55] Iranian leaders also observes that a number of countries with advanced civilian nuclear programmes, like Argentina, Brazil, Israel, Pakistan, and Venezuela refused to agree to the Additional Protocols, but they are not subjected to the same rigorous scrutiny as Iran.[56] Iran feels that the US and the West are making excuses to punish Iran. This argument is advocated by the Conservatives-Radicals Islamists.

Iran argues that the US is seeking excuses to take military action against Iran. President Obama in his speech to the American Israel Public Affairs Committee (AIPAC) in 2012 stated the objective of US policy is "to prevent Iran from obtaining a nuclear weapon."[57] Vice-President Biden reiterated this position to the same audience on 4 March 2013 that the goal of US policy is "to prevent Iran from acquiring a nuclear weapon."[58] US policies under President Obama will be guided by the paramount objective of preventing Iran's acquisition of a nuclear weapon.

Indeed, Iran had produced chemical weapons in the 1980s despite Ayatollah Khomeini's *fatwa*, whether Ayatollah Khamenei's *fatwa* will stop Iran from producing another type of WMD, nuclear arms? This is a very complex question. Ayatollah Khamenei's *fatwa* may be ignored just as Ayatollah Khomeini's was. As of now, the IAEA has not found any evidence suggesting a military aspect to Iran's nuclear activities. But the future is uncertain. Iran may produce nuclear devices in future since Iranian nuclear programme has reached to a stage and acquired capability that it can produce nuclear weapons in the future. Taremi observes that "if the regime finds itself threatened by invasion, it may rush to build a weapon. . . in the guise of a peaceful nuclear programme it may be developing all the elements that would be required to swiftly assemble a nuclear device."[59]

Tarem's observation carries weight since the Islamic Republic has been consistently refusing to stop its nuclear development programme.

Both Conservatives-Radicals and Moderates-Reformists agree the need for self-sufficiency in science and technology. But the differences between the two camps in their approaches to acquisition of science and technology appear that characterises their approaches to the nuclear issue. Both camps agree that Iran must have access to nuclear technology, but they disagree over methods in achieving this ends. The Conservatives-Radicals Islamists argue that development of nuclear programme and its use is necessary since the US and the West have been consistently and persistently threatening Iran.

Both camps agree that it is in the country's interest to acquire nuclear technology and to generate nuclear energy, but they differ in their approaches to accomplish their ends. The Moderates-Reformists are keen to lower tensions with the IAEA, US, and EU by showing country's willingness to cooperate with them and reached an interim deal with them in November 2013 as concluded deals in October 2003 and November 2004 with President Mohammad Khatami. President Rouhani has sought a permanent deal on Iran's nuclear dispute. Negotiations continued and the two sides reached an agreement on 14 July 2015. However, the Conservatives-Radicals, on the other hand claim that the US and EU intend to deny access of nuclear achievement to Iran and seek to impose their hegemony over Iran. As negotiations continue for amicable solution of Iran's nuclear disputes, the different factions appear to have become increasingly active in pushing their positions. The competing factions advocate their different approaches to national security issues like nuclear, a balancing act Ayatollah Khamenei has to play since he has to satisfy all the factions.

However, the decisions over nuclear issue are taken at four levels. First, technical discussions on policy issues takes place in Foreign Ministry and are led by one of the department heads there. Second, substantial debates occur at the Supreme National Security Council (SNSC). Third, a ministerial committee which meetings hold at the SNSC. Fourth, where the decisions are actually taken, is composed of the Supreme Leader,

President, head of the SNSC, the chief nuclear negotiator, and few others.[60] Ultimately, at the fourth level, actual negotiating strategy is determined and important decisions on nuclear policy are taken.

Supreme Leader, Ayatollah Khamenei, is the final arbiter of major decisions like the nuclear issue. But he makes decisions not by decree via a consensus building process involving a small coterie of political institutions and personalities. The Supreme National Security Council, Expediency Council, Council of Guardians, and the Islamic Revolutionary Guard Corps (IRGC) weigh in, and personalities like lead nuclear negotiator, former foreign minister Ali Akbar Velayati (current foreign policy advisor to Ayatollah Khamenei), former presidents Hashemi Rafsanjani and Mahmoud Ahmedinejad are among the principal players. Hard-line ex-President Mahmoud Ahmedinejad is one of the prominent players in determining security issues and he cannot be easily bypassed since he has inserted himself into the debate far more deeper than Iran's earlier president, Mohammad Khatami.

However, Ayatollah Ali Khamenei's personality carries numerous features. One of the major characteristics of his personality is, he has been repeatedly hiding of his views and policies. He rarely issues statements on sensitive issues. The secret nature of Khamenei's real views and policy preferences has confused his supporters and rivals within the political establishment and outside. It actually comes to know much later, what were his policy preferences? For instance, Ayatollah Khamenei's view to the nuclear agreements with the EU-3 (Britain, France, and Germany) and the Atomic Energy Agency (IAEA) in October 2003 and November 2004 on accepting the Additional Protocols and temporary suspension of uranium enrichment were understood as his support for these agreements. In 2012, he strongly condemned the reformists (Khatami faction) and moderates (Rafsanjani faction) for having made those agreements. Ayatollah Khamenei revealed his views and policy preferences only after sidelining the reformists and moderates, and replacing them with the hard-line Mahmoud Ahmedinejad. The political players such as Rafsanjani and the reformists explicitly state their views on policy issues, but Ayatollah Khamenei does not reveal his objectives and preferences. This has been reflecting in pursuit of his foreign policy.

Ahmedinejad successfully brought nuclear policy in public domain and debated thoroughly in Iran which was still confined within ruling elites in Tehran. While Ahmedinejad was president, in all his public meetings and during his provincial visits and addressing rallies raised nuclear issue and made aware people about it, and completely changed security discourse. President Rouhani is bound to pursue a prudent policy pertaining to nuclear issue since it has been a public debate within Iran.

Iran continues to assert that its nuclear programme is purely peaceful, while the US and Israel remain convinced that Tehran is after nuclear bomb. Apparently, general consensus among Russia, China, European countries, and Arab countries is that Iran is after nuclear weapons capability, and the only way to resolve it is direct talks between the US and Iran.

Iran's Foreign Minister Mohammad Javad Zarif under President Rouhani observed in his *Foreign Affairs* (2014) article:

"Iran has no interest in nuclear weapons and is convinced that such weapons would not enhance its security. Iran does not have the means to engage in nuclear deterrence – directly or through proxies – against its adversaries. Furthermore, the Iranian government believes that even a perception that Iran is seeking nuclear weapons is detrimental to the country's security and its regional role, since attempts by Iran to gain strategic superiority in the Persian Gulf would inevitably provoke responses that would diminish Iran's conventional military advantages."[61]

Zarif's observation makes clear that the Islamic Republic is not after nuclear weapons, but suspicions surround around Iran's continued nuclear pursuit efforts.

President Rouhani initiated negotiations on Iran's nuclear dispute with P-5 + 1 (France, Britain, US, Russia, and China, plus Germany) after assuming presidency in August 2013 and reached an interim agreement by November 2013. Mohammad Javad Zarif observes on the interim agreement of the November 2013 that "the goal for these negotiations is to reach a mutually-agreed long-term comprehensive solution that would ensure Iran's nuclear programme will be exclusively peaceful".[62] Finally,

Iran and P-5 + 1 reached an agreement on 14 July 2015. It appears that the Islamic Republic is convinced on one thing that it must ease tensions with the outside world.

Iran's posture on nuclear issue has changed as policy statements illustrate. Indeed, significance of domestic factional politics and their different approaches cannot be denied. In fact, the Supreme Leader, Ayatollah Khamenei, is the ultimate deciding force, and he does not want to alienate one faction completely or to only favour another faction. He allows a certain degree of leeway to the faction 'in power' especially for discussions and actions at the three levels below his office, while continuing to retain ultimate decision-making power himself.[63] He is the final arbiter in the matter of security issues such as nuclear policy.

A diplomatic solution would avoid military strikes against widely dispersed and in many cases well protected Iran's nuclear facilities. Iran has been seeking a negotiated solution to its nuclear dispute since it will receive acceptance of the international community. For Iran, a negotiated solution of nuclear dispute would ease sanctions and offer some degree of validation by the world community. Whether Iran has already decided to build nuclear weapons or not, is a complex question. From the Iranian perception, nuclear deterrence is a necessity.

Consequences of Iranian Nuclear Capability/Weapon

Iran's nuclear development programme has been an issue of contention between Iran and the international community. It has raised concerns not only in the region but also beyond since it has far-reaching implications. The US concerns regarding Iran's nuclear programme are multidimensional - first, a nuclear-armed Iran would pose existential threat to Israel; second, Iran may give these weapons to fundamentalists/terrorists organisations; third, Iran would become more aggressive, assertive, and intimidate its neighbours; and fourth, other countries in the region, particularly Saudi Arabia, Egypt, and Turkey would follow the suit and acquire their own nuclear weapons.[64] However, there is no consensus on these potential threats among policy-makers and analysts.

Iran's possession of nuclear weapons would make the US more hesitant to involve itself in conventional military conflicts in the region. If nuclear arsenals were accompanied by a medium-range ballistic-missile capability, it could threaten the strength of US alliance commitments beyond the region. Development of ballistic missiles could help in increasing Iran's strike capability, and cause heavy damage to the adversary.

The regional countries would respond differently to a nuclear-armed Iran than a nuclear-capable one. Some countries in the region may feel the need to counter Iran's nuclear capability with a nuclear-weapon capability of their own. Apparently "to many in the region, the threat posed by the Iranian nuclear programme stems as much from the prestige and hence influence that it brings to Tehran as from the potential for it to give Iran a military capability".[65] The regional countries view Iranian nuclear programme this way, and seek to develop their own nuclear programmes. In some cases, the countries may not want to pursue their nuclear programme, but may face public pressure to do so.

If Iran acquires nuclear capability, other countries in the region may follow the suit and it will be very difficult to contain nuclear proliferation in the region. The regional countries would like to develop their own nuclear capabilities due to continued Iran's efforts to develop its nuclear capability. Saudi Arabia, Turkey, Jordan, Egypt, the United Arab Emirates (UAE), Oman, Kuwait, Bahrain, and Qatar would like to develop their own nuclear capabilities to counter Iran. However, the responses of these countries vary, but they would seek to protect themselves either developing nuclear their own or getting extended nuclear umbrella to them by someone. In order to contain nuclear proliferation in the region, the US should ensure their security by all means and even extending nuclear umbrella to the region and the regional countries.

Iran's nuclear programme has been viewed by several regional countries as a potential challenge to their security. Saudi Arabia is generally viewed as an adversary of Iran, as evidence by its religious, political, and military challenges for regional dominance.[66] In the light of Iran's quest to develop nuclear capability, the US should ensure security to the region and regional countries by extending nuclear umbrella to them.[67] Saudi

Arabia would seek nuclear deterrence either by developing its own nuclear capability or getting extended nuclear umbrella by the US, or Pakistan. Also, as pointed out in an article by Eric S Edleman, Andrew F Krepinevich, and Evan Braden Montgomery, "The Dangers of a Nuclear Iran", major cultural and religious differences between Saudi Arabia and Iran further complicated the relationship.[68] Edleman and others further point out that the US in not the only place Saudi Arabia would likely look towards as a potential source for a 'nuclear guarantee', it could move toward Pakistan for a nuclear umbrella.[69] Thus, acquisition of nuclear capability/weapon by Iran would have far-reaching implications, even beyond region.

Israel would also respond differently to a nuclear-armed Iran. Israel has long maintained that it will 'not be the first to introduce' nuclear arsenals in the region. It is widely believed that Israel has already acquired nuclear weapons. If Iran declares itself a nuclear power, Israel will do the same. Once Iran declares its nuclear capability then Israel would not only declare itself, but also pursue qualitative and quantitative improvements to its nuclear arms. It would further erode the NPT legitimacy that the region enjoys.

Beyond the region, Iranian move would have far-reaching implications and have serious consequences for global non-proliferation efforts. It would be difficult to garner support for preventing other states from acquiring nuclear weapons too. Therefore, it requires to dissuade Iran from obtaining nuclear capability. Coercive means may not succeed to stop Iran from obtaining nuclear weapons. Military action against Iran would not serve the purpose.

Military action against Iran may not serve purposes and may backfire since Iran's nuclear facilities are hidden, dispersed, and well protected. Military analysts are convinced that these attacks would at best only delay Iran's nuclear programme for two years or so while simultaneously strengthen the position of the Conservative-Radical Islamists in Iran and bolstering their conviction that Iran needs a nuclear deterrence against future military attacks.[70] The Conservatives-Radicals will use it as a tool to suppress internal debates regarding security issues.

Iran has sought to raise the stakes and depicted as a prolonged conflict with unpredictable consequences for uncertain results. Iran stresses the certainty of retaliation, and differentiating Iran from Iraq, Libya, and Syria. Iran's attempts to deter an attack have led to threats to: prolong war; widen hostilities by attacking US bases in the region and the regional states hosting those bases, such as Saudi Arabia and Qatar; disrupt oil traffic in the Persian Gulf; and expand hostilities to include targets outside of West Asia.[71] Thus, military strikes against Iran would have far-reaching implications.

Conclusion

The Revolution 1979 had completely transformed not only polity, society, and foreign policy, but also security policy and issues. Security discourse began following the Revolution and measures were taken to ensure it. Iran's security was defined and redefined since it had departed from the Western security camp. Iran had snapped political, diplomatic, and security ties with the West. The Iran-Iraq War and the United States and the West attitudes towards it had deeply affected the Iranian psyche. The effects of the events had a deep impact over Iran's national security thinking. Iran had to rely on its resources for its defence. The Islamic Republic formed ideological forces and raised the Islamic army to defend, protect, and preserve the Islamic Revolution, the Islamic regime, country's territorial integrity from internal and external threats.

The Islamic Republic changed its arms acquisition policy, restructured the armed forces, and raised units to defend the country. It formed the Islamic army such as Islamic Revolutionary Guard Corps (IRGC) and the Baseji to defend, protect, and preserve the Islamic Revolution and the Islamic regime. The entire forces were restructured and indoctrination in armed-forces was introduced. Ideology was used in raising the armed-forces. Iran's defence doctrine and security strategy is heavily loaded with ideology. Islam played major role in shaping Iran's defence doctrine and security strategy. Thus, Islam has played critical role in shaping national security thinking.

Iran's security perception has been changing since the Revolution 1979. The Islamic Republic had faced different kind of challenges in the

1990s. Therefore, Iran's security requirements changed in the 1990s. Iran felt during Iran-Iraq War that it must develop a 'credible deterrent'. In the process of develop a 'credible deterrent', Iran started nuclear development programme in the 1990s which was halted in the 1980s by Ayatollah Khomeini. Iran completely changed its security policy in the post-Khomeini period. The changing domestic politics in the 1990s and 2000s brought changes in security perception and national security thinking as well. As Iran's security perception changed in the early 2000s, its strategy changed and introduced asymmetric warfare in its defence doctrine.

Factional differences in Iran's security policy appear as polity. The Conservatives-Radicals and the Moderates-Reformist continue to contest over Iran's security policy issues including nuclear policy and strategy, and each pursues different approach to ensure security. Nuclear policy has been consistently debated within political factions/groups about its relevance and the Conservatives-Radicals view nuclear option as necessity. The Conservatives-Radicals Islamists argue in favour of nuclear technology/weapon and have cited historical experiences as reasons. But factional politics remains only at policy levels, and deployment of forces and the battle tactics are spared from political factional influences. Deployment of forces and the battle tactics have been consistently coming under changes as before. Iran has been consistently changing its war strategy. The Moderates-Reformists Islamists differ with the Conservatives-Radicals Islamists on several issues like indoctrination into armed-forces, arms acquisition policy, and nuclear policy.

The variable and invariable factors such as geo-political location, natural resources, economic development, geopolitical developments, developments in the region, and international order have been consistently influencing Iran's security perceptions and national security thinking. Security perceptions of the Conservatives-Radicals differ with the Moderates-Reformists and each pursues different approaches in addressing security issues. Iran's security policy has changed from Ayatollah Khomeini to Hassan Rouhani as the country's behaviours demonstrate. Iran could not adopt a coherent national security policy due to different factional approaches pertaining to security issues. Iran's security policy is largely shaped by domestic situation and political dynamics, including external environment.

Endnotes

1   Barry Buzan, "Security of the States, the New World Order and Beyond", in Ronnie D. Lipschutz, ed., *On Security* (New York: Columbia University Press, 1995), p. 188.

2   Kamran Taremi, "Iranian Strategic Culture: The Impact of Ayatollah Khomeini's Interpretation of Shiite Islam", *Contemporary Security Policy*, vol. 35, no. 1, April 2014, p. 20.

3   Gawdat Bahgat, "The Iranian Nuclear Crisis: An Assessment", *Parameters*, vol. 43, no. 2, Summer 2013, p. 76

4   James K. Sebenius and Michael K. Singh, "Is a Nuclear Deal With Iran Possible?", *International Security*, vol. 37, no. 3, Winter 2012/13, pp 52-91.

5   Steven R Ward, "The Continuing Evolution of Iran's Military Doctrine", *Middle East Journal*, vol. 59, no. 4, Autumn 2005, pp. 65-66.

6   Ibid., p. 66

7   Anoushiravan Ehteshami, "Iran's International Posture After the Fall of Baghdad", *Middle East Journal*, vol. 58, no. 2, Spring 2004, p. 187.

8   Gary Sick, "Trail By Error: Reflections on The Iran-Iraq War", *Middle East Journal*, vol. 43, no. 2, Spring 1989, p. 234

9   R K Ramazani, "Iran's Foreign Policy: Contending Orientations", *Middle East Journal*, vol. 43, no. 2, Spring 1989, p. 214.

10 *Economist* (London), 14 February 1987, p. 30.

11 FBIS-NESA, 7 January 1988, p. 50

12 Ray Takeyh, "Iranian Options: Pragmatic Mullahs and America's Interests", *The National Interests*, Fall 2003, p. 54

13 Jack L Snyder, *The Soviet Strategic Culture: Implications for Limited Nuclear Operations*, RAND R-2154-AF (Santa Monica, California: The RAND Corporation, 1977), p. 8

14 Colin S Gray, "National Styles in Strategy: The American Example", *International Security*, vol. 6, no. 2, Fall 1981, p. 22

15 Ibid.,

16 Colin S Gray, "National Styles in Strategy: The American Example", *International Security*, vol. 6, no. 2, Fall 1981, p. 21-47; and Rashed Uz Zaman, "Strategic Culture: A "Cultural" Understanding of War", *Comparative Strategy*, vol. 28, no. 1, 2009, pp. 68-88

17   Jeffrey S Lantis, "Strategic Culture and National Security Policy", *International Studies Review*, vol. 4, no. 3, Fall 202, pp. 87-113

18   Ruhollah Khomeini, Quwa-ye Musallah dar Andisha-ye Imam Khomeini [The Armed Forces From the Perspective of Ayatollah Khomeini] (Tehran: Mu'assiseh-ye Tanzim va Nashr-e Asar-e Imam Khomeini, 2007), p. 139.

19   Shahram Chubin, *Iran's National Security Policy: Intentions, Capabilities & Impact* (Washington: Carnegie Endowment For International Peace, 1994), p. 18

20   Robert Hewson, "The Sinking Feeling: Iran's Anti-Ship Missile Array", *Rusi Defence Systems*, Summer 2012, pp. 102-03

21   International Institute of Strategic Studies, *Iran's Ballistic Missile Capabilities: A Net Assessment* (London: International Institute of Strategic Studies, 2010), p. 2.

22   For a list of the products produced my the Iranian Defence Industries Organisation, see http://www.diomil.ir/.

23   Muhammad Hussein Jamshidi, *Basis and History of Military Thought in Iran* (Tehran: Islamic Revolutionary Guard Corps College of Command, 2001), pp. 600-604.

24   President Khatami took a soft tone, noted that "The US is deeply engaged in Iraq", *Voice of the IRI Radio I*, 27 August 2004; and Ali Akbar Bareini, "Khatami: Iran is Prepared to Defend itself Against US Attack", *Associated Press*, 20 January 2005

25   "Iranian Pilot Killed While Fighting in Iraq", *Indian Express*, New Delhi, 6 July 2014, p. 20

26   "Iranian Pilot Killed While Fighting in Iraq", *Indian Express*, New Delhi, 6 July 2014, p. 20

27   "Iraqi forces re-captured part of Tikrit from IS", *The Hindu*, Delhi, 12 March, 2015

28   "Iraqi forces re-captured part of Tikrit from IS", *The Hindu*, Delhi, 12 March, 2015; *The Asian Age*, Delhi, 12 March, 2015.

29   See Kamran Taremi, "Iranian Strategic Culture: The Impact of Ayatollah Khomeini's Interpretation of Shiite Islam", *Contemporary Security Policy*, vol. 35, no. 1, April 2014, pp. 3-25; and Steven R Ward, "The Continuing Evolution of Iran's Military Doctrine", *Middle East Journal*, vol. 59, no, 4, Autumn 2005, pp. 559-563

30   "Iran: Complete Regulations of the Islamic Republic of Iran Armed Forces", *Near East and South Asian Supplement*, FBIS-NES-94-208-S, US Foreign

Broadcast Information Service, 27 October 1994.

31 Shahram Chubin, "Is Iran a Military Threat?", *Survival*, vol. 56, no. 2, April-May 2014, p. 79

32 R K Ramazani, *Revolutionary Iran: Challenge and Response in the Middle East* (Baltimore: The Johns Hopkins University Press, 1986), pp. 35-38

33 Ruhollah Khomeini, *Kalamat-e Qaiser: Pand-ha va Hikmat-ha-ye Imam Khomeini* [Short Sentences: Advice and Wise Sayings of Ayatollah Khomeini] (Tehran: Intesharat-e Ilmi va Farhangi, 1993), p. 100

34 Hamid Dabashi, *Shiism: A Religion of Protest* (Cambridge: Harvard University Press, 2011), Part I, pp 73-100

35 Saeid Golkar, "Iran's Revolutionary Guard: Its Views of The United States", *Middle East Policy*, vol. 21, no. 2, Summer 2014, p. 57

36 "Studio Interview with Rear Adm Ali Shamkhani", *Vision of Islamic Republic of Iran (IRI) Network 2*, 28 December, 2000; and "Tehran TV Interviews Defence Minister on Defence Policy", *Vision of Islamic Republic of Iran (IRI) Network 2*, 24 August 2000.

37 Nicola Schahgalidian, *The Iranian Military under the Islamic Republic* (Santa Monica: RAND Corporation, 1987), p. 59

38 Gawdat Bahgat, Nuclear Proliferation: The Islamic Republic of Iran", *Iranian Studies*, vol. 39, no. 3, 2006, pp. 307-327

39 Bahman Baktiari, "Iran's Conservative Revival", *Current History*, vol. 106, no. 696, January 2007, p. 14

40 C Shristine Fair, Karl Kaltenthaler, and William J Miller, "Iranian Bomb: Elite Cues and Support and Opposition to the Development of Nuclear Weapons", *Journal of South Asian and Middle Eastern Studies*, vol. 37, no. 1, Fall 2013, pp. 4-5

41 Kayhan Barzegar, "The Paradox of Iran's Nuclear Consensus", *World Policy Journal*, vol. 26, no. 3, 2009, pp. 21-30

42 Ibid., p. 26

43 Ali Gheissari and Vali Nasr, "The Conservative Consolidation in Iran", *Survival*, vol. 47, no. 2, Summer 2005, p. 186

44 C Christine Fair, Karl Kaltenthaler, and William J Miller, "Iranian Bomb: Elite Cues and Support and Opposition to the Development of Nuclear Weapons", *Journal of South Asian and Middle Eastern Studies*, vol. 37, no. 1, Fall 2013, pp.7-8

45 Fariborz Mokhtari, "No One Will Scratch My Back: Iranian Security

Perceptions in Historical Context", *Middle East Journal*, vol. 59, no. 2, Spring 2005, p. 210

46   Bahman Baktiari, "Iran's Conservative Revival", *Current History*, vol. 106, no. 696, January 2007, p. 15

47   Ali Gheissari and Vali Vasr, "The Conservative Consolidation in Iran", *Survival*, vol. 47, no. 2, Summer 2005, pp. 186-188

48   Ayatollah Khamenei's fatawa on this issue is available at, http://farsi.Khomeini.ir/speech-content?id=3463

49   *Mehr News Agency*, 10 August 2005. Iran conveyed the Supreme Leader's fatwa in an official statement to the IAEA in August 2005.

50   "Iran's Nuclear Theology: Bomb and Truth", *The Economist*, 19 May 2012.

51   Fair, n. 44, pp. 11-12

52   Ibid., p. 15

53   Ibid., p. 17

54   Christopher J Bolan, "The Iranian Nuclear Debate: More Myths Than Facts", *Parameters*, vol. 43, no. 2, Summer 2013, p. 84.

55   Ibid.,

56   Ibid.,

57   Barack Obama, "Remarks by the President at AIPAC Policy Conference", *The White House Office of the Press Secretary*, Washington Convention Center, Washington, DC, 4 March 2012, http://www.whitehouse.gov/the-press-office/2012/03/04/remarks-president-aljac-policy-conference.

58   Joe Biden, "Remarks by the Vice President to the AIPAC Policy Conference", *The White House Office of the Press Secretary*, Washington Convention Center, Washington, DC, 4 March 2013, http://www.whitehouse.gov/the-press-office/2012/03/04/remarks-vice-president-aplac-policy-conference.

59   Taremi, n. 2, p. 14

60   Hassan Rouhani, "Farasou-ye Chalesh-haye Iran va Ajans dar Parvendeh-ye Hasteh-e" (Beyond Iran's Difficulties with the Agency Concerning the Nuclear Issue), *Gofteman*, no. 37, Fall 2005, p. 11

61   Mohammad Javad Zarif, "What Iran Really Wants: Iranian Foreign Policy in the Rouhani Era", *Foreign Affairs*, vol. 93, no. 3, May/June 2014, p. 58

62   Ibid., p. 58

63   Mehran Kamrava, Iranian National Security Debates: Factionalism and Lost

Opportunities", *Middle East Policy*, vol. 14, no. 2, Summer 2007, p. 96.

64 Gawdat Bahgat, "The Iranian Nuclear Crisis: An Assessment", *Parameters*, vol. 43, no. 2, Summer 2013, p. 70

65 Michel A Levi, "Drawing the Line on Iranian Enrichment", *Survival*, vol. 53, no. 4, August-September 2011, p. 191

66 Craig Whitlock and Liz Sly, "For Iran and Saudi Arabia, Simmering Feud is Rotted in History", *The Washington Post*, 11 October 2011, http://articles. washingtonpost.com/2011-10-11/world/35276886_1_saudi-iranian-relations-saudi-arabia-saudi-ambassador

67 Emily Cura Saunders and Bryan L Fearey, "The Least Bad Option? Extending the Nuclear Umbrella to the Middle East", *Comparative Strategy*, vol. 33, no. , pp. 122-130

68 Eric S. Edleman, Andrew F. Krepinevich, and Evan Braden Montgomery, "The Dangers of a Nuclear Iran", *Foreign Affairs*, vol. 90, no. 1, January/February 2011, p. 68

69 Ibid., p. 70

70 Bolan, n. 54, p. 87

71 Shahran Chubin, "Is Iran a Military Threat?", *Survival*, vol. 56, no. 2, April-May 2014, p. 75.

Chapter - 5

Conclusion

Relationship between domestic politics and foreign-security policy began in 1979 that continue to exist. Domestic politics' relation with foreign and security policy and their close ties reflect in Iran's words and deeds and its behaviour. Domestic politics and foreign-security policy established a close relationship in 1979 and remained even after the demise of Ayatollah Khomeini in June 1989. The Revolution of 1979 completely transformed Iran, religion coalesced with politics, and ensued a new political culture. Political factions/groups existed in the 1980s, managed, and survived. But their activities were curtailed by the state in the name of security. Ayatollah Khomeini allowed activities of those political groups who remained supportive to the Islamic Revolution and the Islamic regime. The rise of political factions/groups in the absence of Ayatollah Khomeini added complexity to domestic politics, and changes appeared in the country's behaviour. Alignment and realignment began on ideological lines. Iran experienced bi-polar polity for the first time with the May 1997 presidential elections. The growth of the political factions/groups and their activities have transformed Iran's polity, subsequently affected foreign and security policy despite the *Velayat-e Faqih*. The changes in foreign and security policy appear form Ayatollah Khomeini to Hassan Rouhani due to domestic situation and factional politics.

The event of 1979 in Iran was a long process of political socialisation that culminated into Revolution which replaced monarchy with clerics-rule. Political culture of Iran changed and polity was defined within ambit of religion since the Revolution was led by religious leaders. The leader of the Revolution Ayatollah Khomeini led masses against the Shah and coloured polity with Islam. The dominance of religion during the Revolution had left indelible mark on Iran's society, polity, economy, foreign policy, and security. Religion coalesced with politics, and marked evolution of a different kind of polity in the post-Shah period. The emerging political culture under influence of religion swayed political process. The new political culture in the post-Shah period influenced political process which gave birth to a new kind of political system. The new political system in the post-Shah period influenced state behaviour. The event of 1979 did not transform only Iran's polity, but also foreign policy. As Iran's foreign policy changed in the post-Shah period, security came under stress, and required a new definition. The concept of security was defined and redefined since Iran had departed from western security camp. As Iran departed from western security camp, it had to rely on its own resources to ensure its security.

With changing Iran's political culture in 1979 its pattern of internal and external behaviour changed. Political process began in the post-Shah period under religious influence which affected the state behaviour. Political trends emerged following the Revolution and continued. The political trends - *Rast-e Sunnati, Rast-e Modern, Chap,* and *Rast-e Efrati* – influence/ influenced state behaviour. Debate started on nature and character of polity, political system, social and economic policy, and security issues. Iran's foreign policy remained debatable among the political factions/ groups in general, and Iran-US relationship in particular. The leader of Revolution, Ayatollah Khomeini, considered other factions views in policy formulation, thus managed other political groups.

Ayatollah Khomeini established clerics-rule in Iran with introducing the *Velayat-e Faqih* in political system. The position, status, powers and functions of the *Velayat-e Faqih* are delineated in the constitution which makes it the most powerful institution in the country. This institution in real terms determines polity, foreign policy, defence policy, and security policy. Ayatollah Khomeini ruled over the country despite factional activities and factionalism, and pursued policies as circumstances arose. The current Supreme Leader, Ayatollah Khamenei, is responsible for setting domestic political direction, foreign policy, security policy, defence policy, economic policy, and social issues as his predecessor Ayatollah Khomeini. Thus, this institution continues to play a decisive role in shaping state direction.

Factionalism continued in the 1980s but Ayatollah Khomeini managed all political groups in running the state. Political factions/groups activities increased and intensified after the death of Ayatollah Khomeini and its effects appeared in the domestic politics. Undoubtedly, Ayatollah Khomeini effectively managed political groups and gave direction to the country. With the demise of Ayatollah Khomeini in June 1989, new leadership took charge at Tehran and tried to marginalise other political trends and factions, and succeeded, but could not marginalise for long, and emerged with reformist movement by 1997.

In the early 1990s, politics and the political system was completely dominated by the conservatives but situation gradually changed. Nonetheless, political polarisation on ideological ground started in 1992 with the sacking of Mohammad Khatami as Cultural Minister by President Hashemi Rafsanjani. By the mid-1990s, political polarisation on ideological line strengthened. Political polarisation intensified and divisions took clear shape by 1997. The 1997 presidential elections witnessed vertical division of the political groups into two blocs – the Conservatives-Radicals Islamists and Moderates-Reformists Islamists. Political divisions could not remain with polity, but divisions also appeared at economic, social, foreign policy and security issues.

The May 1997 presidential elections changed Iran in many ways. The immediate effect of the May 1997 presidential election was the emergence of bi-polar polity. Iran experienced a bi-polar polity for the first time with the May 1997 presidential election. The emergence of bi-polar polity in the May 1997 presidential election changed domestic politics, and gave lasting impact over Iran's political system. The alignment and realignment of the political groups began that swayed domestic politics. It is noteworthy that political factions/groups did not stick to a particular bloc/group, and changed their alliances as suited. The fluid nature of Iranian polity continued because of changing alliances of political factions/groups.

Ostensibly Iran's polity is fluid since political factions/groups change their alliances whenever and wherever suits them. As alliances change, effects on domestic politics appear. Generally, domestic politics determines country's direction since political leadership acts according to national pulse. In Iran, domestic politics sets the country's direction but the *Velayat-e Faqih* has to allow and approve that direction. The nation's political pulse also influences the *Velayat-e Faqih*. But it will be an oversimplification to say that domestic politics always determines state policies. The fact remains that the *Velayat-e Faqih* plays the pivot role in determining the state behaviour. The *Velayat-e Faqih* closely monitors domestic politics and day-to-day political development to exercise its options at right moment. The changing domestic politics continues to influence state institutions visibly and invisibly. Thus, the effects of domestic politics over policy options and state behaviour appear in one form and another.

Domestic political dynamics had influenced policy options and state behaviour during Hashemi Rafsanjani (1989-1997), Mohammad Khatami (1997-2005), Mahmoud Ahmedinejad (2005-2013). The result of the June 2013 presidential elections explicitly sketches domestic political dynamics and characteristic of Iranian polity. Domestic political dynamics have been influencing state behaviour in the tenure of President Hassan Rouhani as before. For instance, negotiations on Iran's nuclear dispute with P-5 + 1 (US, Britain France, Russia, China + Germany) were started by Hassan Rouhani which halted during the Ahmedinejad presidency. The influence of domestic politics over policy options and state behaviour began in the Khomeini period which still continues and will be continuing.

The Islamic Republic has been consistently and persistently arguing for independence since the beginning of the Revolution of 1979, and even before the Revolution religious community, nationalists, leftists, and liberals criticised Shah's foreign policy. Iran's engagement with the outside world during the Shah and its effects on polity, economy, society, and culture united opposition against the Shah. As domestic politics changed, the new government reversed the Shah's foreign policy orientation and objectives, and ruptured relations with the outside world in order to become independent. In the post-Shah period, the context of Iran's relations with the outside world changed. Ayatollah Khomeini set agenda of the country and pursued a new foreign policy which isolated Iran regionally and globally. Domestic political situation and political dynamics played vital role in formulation of the post-Revolution foreign policy. Iran's foreign policy witnessed a complete change and continued thereafter with slight modification. In the beginning, Ayatollah Khomeini ruptured Iran's relations with the outside world but later changed his stance. He began to normalise Iran's relations with selected countries which was carried on by Hashemi Rafsanjani.

The Iran-Iraq War ceasefire in July 1988, demise of Ayatollah Khomeini in June 1989, and economic reconstruction, brought changes in Iran's attitudes towards the outside world. A confrontational foreign policy towards both the East and the West of the 1980s had been abandoned. President Hashemi Rafsanjani (1989-1997) offered conciliatory messages to the world and pursued the engagement policy as a foreign policy approach. Rafsanjani sought engagement with the outside world. Rafsanjani's offers were not as respected in the West, especially in the United States, as Iran expected. The United States imposed sanctions against Iran in the mid-1990s that put President Hashemi in a bizarre situation. The US action discouraged the Rafsanjani Administration and its rapprochement policy. Rafsanjani initiated process of reconciliation and interactions with the outside world, but also took into account domestic political dynamics. The Conservatives-Radicals Islamists remained suspicious to the United States and the West. The US sanctions against Iran was played out against Rafsanjani by the conservatives and radicals. Rafsanjani stressed on Iran's 'Look East' policy and expanded as the US imposed sanctions, although consideration began to improve relations with the eastern countries while Ayatollah Khomeini was alive. Rafsanjani expanded relations with China, Pakistan, India, Japan, North Korea, and other Asian countries. Actually Rafsanjani began moderation in Iran's foreign policy that was continued and expanded by Mohammad Khatam.

President Mohammad Khatami (1997-2005) continued the previous government's policies and further expanded Iran's relations with the outside world. His moderate policy paid dividend, and Iran's relations with the outside world improved. As Khatami consolidated his power, increased interactions with the outside world. Iran's acceptability regionally and globally increased during Khatami period. As domestic political situation changed, visible changes appeared in Iran's foreign policy during Khatami period as Rafsanjani. Khatami gave boost to Iran's 'Look East' policy which was pursued by his predecessor, Hashemi Rafsanjani. Khatami further expanded Iran's relations with China, Pakistan, India, Japan, North Korea, and other Asian countries.

Khatami made efforts to improve Iran's relations with the outside world that yielded some tangible results. He improved Iran's relations with the regional countries and the West. Iran's relations with Saudi Arabia and other Gulf countries also improved. Khatami cooperated with the US in overthrowing the Taliban government in November 2001 and shared intelligence. The Bush Administration designated Iran as 'Axis of Evils' in 2002 that discouraged Khatami and his supporters. Furthermore, the US sanctioned funds for regime change in Tehran in 2005. Thus, the Bush Administration discouraged the Khatami Administration and alienated Iran from the US. The US policies towards Iran provided opportunity to the Conservatives-Radicals to target Khatami.

Mohammad Khatami's praise to the Western civilisation did not go well in the establishment since clerics struggled against the Shah to free Iran from the United States and West, and they ruptured ties with the US following the Revolution of 1979 in order to maintain their independence. His view on the Western civilisation was a break from Iran's cultural, religious, and social values which organised and intensified clerical opposition against him. He maintained distance from clerics by praising the Western civilisation to which Iran must look without prejudice while declaring that the West's political system was not flawless. This provided opportunity to the Conservatives-Radicals Islamists to unite against the moderates, and political groups organised and reorganised on ideological lines. Khatami could not reform Iran politically, socially, and economically as expected, and this was attributed to his failure. Moreover, Mohammad Khatami's nuclear agreement with the EU-3 (Britain, France, and Germany) in October 2003 and November 2004 did not go well in the establishment. In the June 2005 presidential elections, Mahmoud Ahmedinejad won by defeating the ex-President Hashemi Rafshanjani.

In Iran's political system, the president has to carry the wishes of the *Velayat-e Faqih,* since latter is the leader of the nation. The confrontation between the two institutions would curtail the president's ability to function. Khatami avoided confrontational approach and pursued accommodation policy. Confrontational policy would have curtailed Khatami's ability to implement some policies. Therefore, Khatami avoided confrontation with the Supreme Leader, Ayatollah Khamenei. Khatami initiated policies which had far-reaching impact over Iran's political system and the society as a whole.

President Ahmedinejad (2005-2013) reversed previous policies, and pursued a different diplomacy. He was critical to the West, the United States, and Israel, and criticised their attitudes towards Iran. Ahmedinejad pursued pro-active regional policy, and deepened Iran's involvement in the region, thus strengthened 'strategic depth' in the Arab. His Gulf policy antagonised the regional countries and the US as well. Although Mohammad Khatami started to increase Iran's activities in the region in general, and Iraq in particular, was further expanded by his successor. Ahmedinejad adopted confrontational foreign policy as the Iranian leadership pursued in the 1980s. His confrontational foreign policy delved Iran into international isolation, consequently economy was severely affected. The efforts of Rafsanjani and Khatami got a severe jolt, actually halted by Ahmedinejad. President Ahmedinejad's domestic policies brew tension within Iran and political groups/factions started to organise and reorganise to challenge him.

The June 2009 presidential elections and controversy over its result marked changing domestic politics. This event set direction of Iranian polity since Ahmedinejad's opponents were also seeking an opportunity to target him. The crack appeared within the conservatives groups after the 2009 presidential elections and the gap between Ahmedinejad and the conservatives increased. The political groups/factions began to organise and reorganise as before. By 2012, domestic politics changed and convergence of interests between Rafsanjani faction and the Moderates-Reformists appeared. Rafsanjani faction and Moderates-Reformists narrowed down their differences and extended support to Hassan Rouhani in the June 2013 presidential elections. It is noteworthy that a section of the conservatives also extended support to Hassan Rouhani. Rouhani won the presidential elections of the June 2013 with their support, and succeeded Mahmoud Ahmedinejad.

The disillusionment of the people and economic difficulties caused the rise of dissent voices against Ahmedinejad. Ahmedinejad's confrontational foreign policy isolated Iran regionally and globally. Iran's regional and international isolation and economic sanctions provided space and opportunity for the rise of moderate voices during the Ahmedinejad period. The Moderates-Reformists took advantage of the situation and criticised the Conservatives-Radicals and targeted Ahmedinejad. As Iran faced economic pressure, debate began on the relevance of confrontational foreign policy. Alignment and realignment among political factions/ groups began in the society. As Iran's domestic politics changes, shifts in foreign policy appear too.

President Rouhani has been pursuing the 'engagement' policy with the outside world since Ahmedinejad's confrontational foreign policy isolated Iran regionally and globally. Rouhani's foreign policy approach differs from the previous administration. Ahmedinejad's confrontational foreign policy caused sanction one after another which created pressure over Iran's economy. He seeks to maintain relations with the foreign countries and has offered conciliatory messages to the world. President Rouhani follows moderation, conciliation, and accommodation in his foreign policy approach to break Iran's regional and global isolation. Domestic situation and political dynamics plays a major role in shaping Iran's foreign policy since composition of support base changes. Iran's policy of de-internationalisation has caused a gradual decline in infrastructure, near the absent of foreign investment, political irrelevance, and technological obsolescence.

Domestic politics continues to influence state behaviour as before. The Moderates-Reformists seek engagement with the outside world to increase Iran's acceptability in the international community. The Moderates-Reformists pursue rapprochement, accommodation, and engagement policy with the outside world. The real challenge facing the Moderates-Reformists today lies in their persuading the Conservatives-Radicals to accept this conception as a principle of Iran's foreign policy. The Moderates-Reformists can demonstrate the inescapable reality of the fusion of the world culture, a culture marked by the advancement of science and technology and an insatiable quest for economic betterment, social justice and political freedom that knows no boundaries. For instance, both China and Russia tried to reject the concept of an interdependence world culture, but finally both accepted it. They had no other choice, nor does Iran.

As far as Iran-United States relation is concerned, deliberations have been continued. The Revolution of 1979 completely transformed Iran's polity and consequently changed the Iran-US relationship context. In 1979 and 1980, Iran-US relationship defined and redefined that had far-reaching implications. The bellicose of Iran in the early 1980s against the US did not continue for long but, the two countries remained hostile to each other. The hostility between Iran and the US began in the 1980s continued and their relationship remained adversarial.

In domestic politics, Iran-United States relationship has remained centre of debate since the Revolution of 1979. Shah's pro-US policy was depicted by the Islamists in the 1960s, 1970s, and 1980s as a source of evil. The US was the most hated in Iran in the 1970s and 1980s. For the United States, the implications of the Islamic Revolution suggests a need for the US to come to terms with the fact that some of Iran's hostile words and deed are a direct result of Washington's own misguided policies both before and after the Revolution. In fact, the eruption of Revolution itself in part reflected alienation from the US, most of all popular perception that it was smothering Iran's sense of dignity and independence by its military, economy and political support of the Shah's regime and Washington's support to his repressive rule. Iran-US mistrust developed before the Revolution that continued the post-Revolution period.

The sense of mistrust that developed in the 1950s, 1960s, 1970s, 1980s, and 1990s still continues in Iran's memory. Iranian leadership remains sceptical to the US intentions towards the Islamic regime and Iran. The Islamic Republic tried to improve ties with the United States in the 1990s. President Bill Clinton's 'Dual Containment' (Iran and Iraq) policy in 1992 alienated Iran form the US. The enmity increased as Washington imposed economic sanctions against Iran in 1994 and 1995. The US policies had deeply affected Iran's domestic politics, thus influenced national security thinking.

The mistrust that developed between Iran and US in the past, cannot easily disappear. The past experiences continue to haunt in Iran's memories and play role in determining Tehran-Washington relationship. However, Iran-US relations can be maintained if both realise their interests. In order to restore Iran-US relations, the Moderates-Reformists need to broaden and deepen their support base among the people. The US needs to place its relations with Iran on a plan of reciprocal interests and mutual respect. President Rouhani has been exploring ways to maintain a working relationship with the United States since Ahmedinejad's confrontational foreign policy increased bitterness between the two countries.

Iran-United States relations have remained an area of contest between the two groups since the 1980s, and each is pulling in the opposite direction as before. Iran's foreign policy faced pressures in the early period of the Revolution and witnessed almost reversal initial few years of the Revolution. The debate on Iran's foreign policy has been continued between the conservatives and the moderates, and there is no unanimity on various issues among the leaders. Indeed, the debate has curtailed ability of the Iranian leadership to adopt a coherent foreign policy.

The current debate between the Conservatives-Radicals and the Moderates-Reformists – like earlier debates between the revolutionary Islamists and the revolutionary nationalists on the nature of Iran's foreign policy - reveals the still unresolved underlying differences. Yet, Iran's experience over the decades has produced new ideas that may point the way for Iran to come to terms in foreign policy without sacrificing its Islamic ideals. Iran's foreign policy continues to pursue Islamic ideals, simultaneously expands relations in other areas. Islamic ideals have remained in pursuit of Iran's foreign policy since religion has coalesced with politics.

Iran has maintained its relations with Russia despite Russia's offensive operations against Muslim separatists of Chechnya. It illustrates that the voices of Moderates in foreign policy are not ignored. Iran continues to support the Palestinian issue and has stated so many times about Israel's usurpation of Muslim land. Iran supports *Hezb-e Allah* and *Hamas* against Israel for liberation of Palestinian land which is occupied by Israel. As such

Iran has not yet abandoned Islamic ideals in pursuit of its foreign policy but continues to expand its relations with outside world. The aim of Iran's domestic and foreign policy is to protect and guard Islamic Revolution, the *Velayat-e Faqih*, and Islamic ideals and values. Iran's foreign policy continues to defend Islamic values since they are entwined with Iran's security. Domestic politics continues to influence foreign and security policy since religion has mingled with politics. The fusion of religion with politics in 1979 changed Iran's security perception and national security thinking.

The Revolution of 1979 did not only rupture political and diplomatic relations with the West and the United States, but also economic ties. Iran's trade with the Western countries and the US curtailed and became negligible as these countries imposed sanctions. The West and the United States imposed economic sanctions against Iran in the 1980s which suffered Iranian economy. Economic sanctions caused shortages of essential commodities and defence items in Iran. It also curtailed Iran's ability to buy arms in international market. Iran was forced to buy arms and other commodities at higher prices, and less desirable substitutes, in third-party markets.

The United States and the West sanctions against Iran did not only affect economy, but also curtailed Iran's ability to purchase arms in international market. Undoubtedly, Iran's defence purchase ability was curtailed due to economic sanctions. Iran received arms and ammunitions from China and the United States in the 1980s despite economic sanctions. In the 1990s and onwards Iran obtained arms and ammunitions from China, Russia, North Korea, and other sources.

However, the majority of bilateral oil and gas agreements involving capital investment or transfer of technology have been effectively blocked by sanctions and US pressures. US sanctions have changed the situation for Iranian business by adversely affecting the country's terms of trade, and raising the cost of foreign capital for development financing. Moreover, Iran's defence agreements and transfers of sensitive technology with other countries are also blocked by sanctions and US pressures. The US action further alienated Iran and Iranian people from the US.

The effects of economic sanctions appeared at Iran's domestic politics. Sanctions raised nationalistic fervour, strengthened the regime's legitimacy and increased power bases. Apparently sanctions helped in modifying Iran's political posture to some extent. In nutshell, sanctions help/helped in strengthening the regime's legitimacy and modify the political posture to some extent. It appears that when external forces applied sanctions, it created difficulties for the Iranian economy and posed challenges for the regime, but it also served to keep the regime in power beyond its time. Universal enmity may have the unintended consequence of arousing the people's sense of patriotism where survival at any cost may become a stronger instinct. Any declared intention to isolate and destabilise Iran is played into the Conservatives-Radicals Islamists' hands, and strengthened nationalistic sentiments and solidarity.

The people felt economic hardship in the 1980s, Iran modified its behaviour. Ayatollah Khomeini modified the country's external behaviour and opened Iran's relations with some foreign countries. Ahmedinejad's policy caused sanctions one after another, consequently Iranian economy suffered. President Rouhani seeks 'constructive engagement' with the outside world to ease sanctions and avoid economic hardship. It appears that Rouhani has modified political posture to ease economic pressure. Apparently the changes in Iran's behaviour seem to break international isolation and avoid economic difficulties. Economic hardship may become a deciding factor in changing Iran's behaviour only when nationalistic elements within politically active population are convinced that Iran's territorial integrity and sovereignty will not suffer by the sanctions and the US enmity.

The Revolution of 1979 did not change only Iran's polity and foreign policy, but also security policy. Iran's security perception changed in the early 1980s as it departed from western security camp. The Iran-Iraq War has had deep impact over national security thinking. Iran-US relationship continues to affect Iran's security perception since the two countries are still adversary. Iran-US enmity began in the 1980s which continues and the two countries have not yet resolved their differences. Moreover, the West and the United States' attitudes towards Iran in general and during Iran-Iraq War in particular, had impact over Iran's security perception and national security thinking. Iran is very sensitive on foreign issues. Domestic politics witnesses changes when foreign countries try/tried to target Iran.

The United States and the West raised questions over political legitimacy of the regime and have reiterated again and again. Iranian leadership draws conclusion that the US and the West seek to change regime in Iran and have been consistently making efforts in this direction. The United States and the West words and deeds have influenced national security thinking. Iran views its security in terms of territorial and ideological security. Thus, survival of the Islamic regime is the prime concern of Iranian leadership. Iran will make all efforts to protect and safeguard the Islamic regime which was born out of the 1979 Revolution. It has adopted military doctrine to defend and protect Iran's territory and Islamic regime.

Iran adopted military doctrine in the early 1990s though it began to evolve in the 1980s. The evolved military doctrine is based on Iran's security perceptions. Iran's security perceptions have been changing since the Revolution 1979 because of regional and global situations. Iran formally adopted military doctrine in the early 1990s though its evolution started in the 1980s. Iran had different security requirements in the 1990s and did not continue the same as had in the 1980s. The military doctrine was adopted and codified in 1992 in the regulations of the Iranian armed forces. Actually, the regulations were an attempt to build on wartime experiences, military ongoing missions and evolution of threats from actual and potential enemies. The doctrine puts emphasis on self-reliance, conventional weapons, ballistic missile based deterrence, nuclear option, unconventional operations, Iran's strategic depth and popular mobilisation of warfare. The Islamic Republic also developed post-war doctrine due to losses of men and weapons during the Iran-Iraq War and the success of US efforts to restrict weapons sales to Iran. When the basic principles of Iranian military and strategy doctrine were adopted in 1992, Iran lacked weapons, technology and basic resources, but had to rely on geography, manpower resources, nationalistic and revolutionary fervour.

Iran's national security policy is defensive and will remain defensive. Its military posture is defensive. It has developed its military doctrine in order to defend the Islamic Revolution and country's boundary. Iranian forces is restructured and repeatedly declared defensive. Iran's goals are to protect and preserve national independence, territorial integrity, regional interests, and the *Velayat-e Faqih*. Iran's military capabilities are limited, so, it has pursued a deterrence-based doctrine that stresses an adversary's risks and costs. Iran's concept of war seeks to avoid conventional military conflict, especially with the US, and rely on regular warfare and asymmetric warfare. For asymmetric warfare, Iran needs to mobilise manpower and capital that requires domestic political support. Domestic situation continues to influence security perception that shape in evolving military doctrine. As far as Iran is concerned, politics and religion has a complex relationship. They have coalesced and cannot be separated. Thus, Islam plays critical role in shaping defence policy and national security thinking.

As Islam played crucial role in deciding direction of Iranian polity, it also determined national security issues. Islam is most felt at the level of national security objectives, military objectives, and to a lesser extent at the level of operational strategy. Islam influences battlefield strategy. Ideology is one of the basic and most important ingredients in regime's prioritising threats to national security. Ideological threats are serious threats to Iran which Iran's leaders fear most. The threats posed by the rival cultures have different set of values from those of Islam. As an ideology, Islam has deeply influenced strategic culture of Iran. The fusion of religion with politics reflects that Islam has deeply affected Iranian strategic culture. Indeed, Islam has deep influence on Iran's world view and action plan.

As domestic politics and external environment changed in the 1990s and 2000s, perceptible changes appeared in Iran's national security and its requirements. Forces were restructured, and raised new forces to safeguard the Islamic Revolution and the Islamic regime. But these remained under constant political pressures due to various political factions/groups and their different perceptions and approaches on security issues. The recruitment in forces remained issues of debate within political groups/ factions, and they were divided. However, factional politics has remained only at policy levels, and deployment of forces and the battle tactics are spared from political factional influences. Deployment of forces and the battle tactics have been consistently coming under changes as before. Iran has been consistently changing its war strategy with deploying new arms and ammunitions. Security issues have remained debate among the political factions/groups and each pursues different approach in ensuring the regime security and territory integrity.

Nuclear policy is one of the most important issues which intensely debated among political factions/groups and the people in Iran. It has been consistently debated within the two camps about its relevance and in ensuring Iran's security. The relevance of Iran's nuclear programme has been issue of debate within political factions/groups. The Conservatives-Radicals views that nuclear option would ensure Iran's security whereas the Moderates-Reformists argues that use of nuclear weapons during wars is out of question since world is interdependence. The Moderates-Reformists advocate that Iran should concentrate on economic development and acquire advance technology. It reflects that domestic politics influences security issues including nuclear policy. Ahmedinejad's contribution to nuclear debate cannot be overlooked since he drew it into public domain which was remained within elites. Nuclear debate within Iran demonstrates that Iranian polity carries diverse political forces and views.

The Conservatives-Radicals Islamists and Moderates-Reformists Islamists have been consistently debating security issues and policy, however each pursues different approach in addressing security issues. Iran could not adopt a coherent national security policy due to different factional approaches pertaining to security policy and issues. Iran's foreign policy has also remained an issue of debate between the two blocs and unanimity has not yet evolved on foreign policy issues such as Iran-US relationship.

The Conservatives-Radicals Islamists favours continuation of nuclear programme and argues that Iran's nuclear technology/weapons would provide security to it since the West and the US have been issuing threat again and again. Therefore, this section argues for nuclear option. No doubt, nuclear deterrence may become an option in future as Iran masters nuclear technology and builds facilities that will allow it to go nuclear. It is noteworthy that Iranian strategic culture allows the right to pre-emption if an attack is imminent. As the US and Israel have been threatening to strike over Iran's nuclear sites and facilities then the Islamic Republic can exercise pre-empt policy. Iran has not yet exercised pre-emption right despite serious challenges. Evidently, Iran's defence policy is defensive and seems to continue. The past experiences illustrate that Iran never used its defence capability for offensive purposes despite provocations.

In Iran's nuclear disputes, Tehran and Washington are undoubtedly the two most important players in the equation. Moreover, political decisions taken by the outside actors will play a critical role in determining future of Iran's nuclear programme. Iran's nuclear programme is a conflict potential that international community seeks to resolve. In Iran, a large section supports for nuclear technology/weapons in order to ensure security. President Rouhani started negotiations with the UN Security Council, the US, and the European countries to resolve Iran's nuclear dispute, and reached an interim agreement with them in November 2013. The negotiations between Iran and the P-5 + 1 continued, and finally the two sides signed an agreement on 14 July 2015. Mahmoud Ahmedinejad started uranium enrichment process and nuclear activities which was voluntarily and temporarily suspended by Mohammad Khatami under Iran and EU-3 (Britain-France-Germany) nuclear agreements of October 2003 and November 2004. It clearly demonstrates that each administration modifies previous administration's policy. The behaviour of the state reflects that domestic politics influences nuclear policy, and will be continuing. Besides domestic situation, other factors also influence Iran's defence policy, security policy, and security issues.

Size, topography, geo-strategic location, natural resources, economic development, geopolitics, developments in the region, and international order have been consistently playing role in shaping Iran's security perceptions, security strategy, and foreign policy. These invariable and variable factors remain feature in influencing national security thinking. They impinge on Iran's national security. They play an important role in building security perception and security strategy.

In political, economic, foreign policy, security arenas, oscillation has been pattern from one administration to the next and even within administrations as they experiment with diverse approaches. The pattern of interactions changes from one administration to the next because of domestic situation, political dynamics, and changing factional equations. Policy differences appear/appeared from one administration to the next. Domestic situation and political factions/groups have been playing a decisive role in shaping state behaviour, and will continue to do so. Iran's behaviours illustrate that its foreign-security policy is a mirror image of 'domestic politics'. Iran's foreign and security policy has been shaped largely by domestic situation including factional politics, and external environment.

Bibliography

Books

Persian Sources

Bazargan, Mohandes Mehdi, *Enqalab-e Iran dar Dau Harkat* [The Iranian Revolution in Two Phases] (Tehran: Chap-e Sevom, 1362 [1983-84])

Khomeini, Ruhollah, *Quwa-ye Musallah dar Andisha-ye Imam Khomeini* [The Armed Forces From the Perspective of Imam Khomeini] (Tehran: Mu'assiseh-ye Tanzim va Nashr-e Asar-e Imam Khomeini, 2007)

Kalamat-e Qaiser: Pand-ha va Hikmat-ha-ye Imam Khomeini [Short Sentences: Advice and Wise Sayings of Imam Khomeini] (Tehran: Intesharat-e Ilmi va Farhangi, 1993)

Malekzadeh, M., *Tarikh-e Enqlab-e Mashrutiyat-e Iran*, Vols. 6 and 7 (Tehran: Elmi, 1373/1994)

English Sources

Alexander, Yonah and Milton Hoenig, *The New Iranian Leadership: Ahmedinejad, Terrorism, Nuclear Ambition, and the Middle East* (Westport: Praeger Security International, 2008)

Ansari, Ali M, *Iran, Islam and Democracy: The Politics of Managing Change* (London: Catham House, 2006), *Confronting Iran: The Failure of American Foreign Policy And The Roots of Mistrust* (London: C. Hurst and Co. Ltd, 2006)

Ansari, M. Hamid, (ed), *Iran Today: Twenty Five Years After the Islamic Revolution* (New Delhi: Rupa Co, 2005)

Anthony H. Cordesman, *The Gulf and the West: Strategic Relations and Military Realities* (London Westview Press, 1988)

Chubin, Shahram, *Iran's National Security Policy: Intentions, Capabilities and Impact* (Washington: Carnegie Endowment For International Peace, 1994)

Clawson, Patrick and Michael Rubin, (eds), *Eternal Iran: Continuity and Chaos* (New York: Palgrave, 2005)

Cordesman, Anthony H., *The Gulf and the West: Strategic Relations and Military Realities* (London: Westview Press, 1988)

Cordesman, Anthony H and Marti Kleiber, (eds), *Iran's Military Forces and Warfighting Capabilities: The Threat in the Northern Gulf* (London: Praeger Security International, 2007)

Dabashi, Hamid, *Shiism: A Religion of Protest* (Cambridge: Harvard University Press, 2011)

Ehteshami, Anoushiravan and Mahjoob Zweiri, (eds.), *Iran and the Rise of its Neoconservatives: The Politics of Tehran's Silent Revolution* (New York: I B Tauris, 2007)

Eposito, John L and R K Ramazani, (eds), *Iran at the Crossroads* (New York, Palgrave, 2001)

Gheissari, Ali and Vali Nasr, *Democracy in Iran: History and the Quest for Liberty* (New York: Oxford University Press, 2006)

Holliday, Shabnam J, *Defining Iran: Politics of Resistance* (Farnham: Ashgate Publishing Ltd, 2011)

Jamshidi, Muhammad Hussein, *Basis and History of Military Thought in Iran* (Tehran: Islamic Revolutionary Guard Corps College of Command, 2001)

Keddie, N R, *Modern Iran: Roots and Results of Revolution* (New Haven: Yale University Press, 2003)

Kile, Shannon N., *Perspectives on Non-Proliferation* (New York: Oxford University Press, 2005)

Lowe, Robert and Claire Spencer, eds., *Iran, Its Neighbours And The Regional Crises* (Chatham House, 2006)

Martin, Vanessa, *Creating an Islamic State: Khomeini and the Making of a New Iran* (London: I B Tauris, 2003)

Menashri, David, *Post-Revolutionary Politics in Iran: Religion, Society and Power* (London: Frank Cass, 2001)

Moslem, Mehdi, *Factional Politics in Post-Khomeini Iran* (New York: Syracuse University Press, 2002)

Omid, Homa, *Islam and the Post-Revolutionary State in Iran* (London: Macmillan Press, 1994)

Panah, Maryam, *The Islamic Republic and the World: Global Dimensions of the Iranian Revolution* (London: Pluto Press, 2007)

Pollack, M Kenneth, *The Persian Puzzle: The Conflict Between Iran and America* (New York: Random House, 2004)

Ramazani, R K, *The Foreign Policy of Iran 1500-1941: A Developing Nation in World Affairs* (Charlottesville: University Press of Virginia, 1966); *Revolutionary Iran: Challenges and Response in the Middle East* (Baltimore: The Johns Hopkins University Press, 1986)

Ridgeon, Lioyd, (ed), *Religion and Politics in Modern Iran* (London: I B Tauris, 2005)

Schahgalidian, Nicola, *The Iranian Military under the Islamic Republic* (Santa Monica: RAND Corporation, 1987)

Venter, Al J, *Iran's Nuclear Option: Tehran's Quest for the Atom Bomb* (Philadelphia: Casemate, 2005)

Articles

Abbas William Samii, Dissent in Iranian Elections: Reasons and Implications", *Middle East Journal*, vol. 58, no. 3, Summer 2004

Abdul Rahman Ansari, "The "Street" And Political Elite in Iran: Reflections On The 2009 Iranian Presidential Elections", *World Affairs*, vol. 14, no.

1, Spring 2010

Afshon Ostovar, "Iran's Basij: Membership in a Militant Islamist Organisation" *Middle East Journal*, vol. 67, no. 3, Summer 2013

Akbar Ganji, "Who Is Ali Khamenei?: The Worldview of Iran's Supreme Leader", *Foreign Affairs*, vol. 92, no. 5, September/ October 2013

Ali Gheissari and Vali Nasr, "The Conservative Consolidation in Iran", *Survival*, vol. 47, no. 2, Summer 2005

Ali M Ansari, Iran Under Ahmedinejad: The Politics of Confrontation", *Adelphi Paper 393* (London: IISS)

Ali Rahigh-Aghsan and Peter Viggo Jakobsen, "The Rise of Iran: How Durable, How Dangerous?", *Middle East Journal*, vol. 64, no. 4, Autumn 2010

Amin Saikal, "The Roots of Iran's Election Crisis", *Survival*, vol.51, no.5, October-November 2009

Anoushirvan Ehteshami, "The Rise and Impact of Iran's Neocons", *The Stanley Foundation*, April 2008

Anthony Parsons, "Iran And Western Europe", *Middle East Journal*, vol. 43, no. 2, Spring 1989

Bahman Baktiari, "Iran's Conservative Revival", *Current History*, vol. 106, no. 696, January 2007

Banafshah Keynoush, "Iran After Ahmedinejad", *Survival*, vol. 54, no. 3, June-July 2012

Bernard Hourcade, "The Rise to Power of Iran's Guardians of the Revolution", *Middle East Policy*, vol.16, no.3, Fall 2009

C. Christine Fair, Karl Kaltenthaler and William J Millar, "Iranians and the Bomb: Elite Cues and Support and Opposition to the Development of Nuclear Weapons", *Journal of South Asian and Middle Eastern Studies*, vol. 37, no. 1, Fall 2013

Christopher J. Bolan, The Iranian Nuclear Debate: More Myths Than Facts",
Parameters, vol. 43, no. 2, Summer 2013

Clifton W Sherrill, "Who Will Succeed Iran's Supreme Leader", *Orbis*, vol.
55, no. 4, Fall 2011; "Why Hassan Rouhani Won Iran's 2013 Presidential
Election", *Middle East Policy*, vol. 21, no. 2, Summer 2014

Colin S. Gary, "National Style in Strategy: The American Example"
International Security, vol. 6, no. 2, Fall 1981

D. Brumberg, "Dissonant Politics in Iran and Indonesia", *Political Science
Quarterly*, vol. 116, no. 3, 2001

Eric Hooglund, "Iranian Views of Arab-Arab Israeli Conflict", *Journal of
Palestinian Studies,* vol. 25, no. 1, Autumn 1995

Fariborz Mokhtari, "No One Will Scratch My Back: Iranian Security
Perceptions in Historical Context", *Middle East Journal*, vol. 59, no. 2,
Spring 2005

Gary Sick, "Trail By Error: Reflections On The Iran-Iraq War, *Middle East
Journal*, vol. 43, no. 2, Spring 1989

Gawdat Bahgat, "The Iranian Nuclear Crisis: An Assessment", *Parameters*,
vol. 43, no. 2, Summer 2013; "Nuclear Proliferation: The Islamic
Republic of Iran, Iranian Studies", vol. 39, no. 3, 2006; "Iran-Turkey
Energy Cooperation: Strategic Cooperation", *Middle East Policy*, vol.
21, no. 4, Winter 2014; "Iran's Relations with Persian Gulf Arab States
– Implications for the United States", *Journal of South Asian and Middle
Eastern Studies*, vol. 38, no. 2, Winter 2015

Ghani Jafar, "Iran Elections: a resounding victory for President
Ahmedinejad", *Strategic Studies*, vol.29, nos. 2 and 3, Summer and
Autumn 2009; "Iranian Nuclear Crisis and the Gulf Sheikhdoms",
Strategic Studies, vol. 28, nos. 2 and 3, Summer and Autumn 2008

Hossein Seifzadeh, "The Landscape of Factional Politics in Iran", *The
Middle East Journal*, vol. 57, no.1, Winter 2003

Jaeques E C Hymans, "Botching the Bomb", *Foreign Affairs*, vol. 91, no. 3,
May-June 2012

Jahangir Amuzegar, "Ahmedinejad's Legacy", *Middle East Policy*, vol. 20, no. 4, Winter 2013; "Islamic Social Justice, Iranian Style", *Middle East Policy*, vol. 14, no. 3, Fall 2007; "The Amhadinejad Era: Preparing For The Apocalypse", *Journal of International Affairs*, vol. 60, no. 2, Spring/ Summer 2007; "Khatami's Legacy: Dashed Hopes", *Middle East Journal*, vol. 60, no. 1, Winter 2006; "Iran's 20-Year Economic Perspective: Promises and Pitfalls", *Middle East Policy*, vol.16, no.3, Fall 2009 ; "The Islamic Republic of Iran: Facts and Fiction", *Middle East Policy*, vol. 19, no. 1, Spring 2012; "Khatami And The Iranian Economy At Mid-Term", *Middle East Journal*, vol. 53, no. 4, Autumn 1999; "Iran's Economy And The US Sanctions", *Middle East Journal*, vol. 51, no. 2, Spring 1997

James A Bill, "Power and Religion in Revolutionary Iran", *Middle East Journal*, vol. 36, no. 1, Winter 1982

James K Sebenius and Michael K. Singh, "Is a Nuclear Deal With Iran Possible?", *International Security*, vol. 37, no. 3, Winter 2012/13

Jeffrey S Lantis, "Strategic Culture and National Security Policy", *International Studies Review*, vol. 4, no. 3, Fall 2002

Kamran Taremi, "Iranian Strategic Culture: The Impact of Ayatollah Khomeini's Interpretation of Shiite Islam", *Contemporary Security Policy*, vol. 35, no. 1, April 2014

Karim Sadjapour, "The Nuclear Players", *Journal of International Affairs*, vol. 60, no. 2, Spring/Summer 2007

"How Relevant is the Iranian Street?", *The Washington Quarterly*, vol. Vol. 30, no. 1, 2007

Kayhan Barzegar, "Iran's Foreign Policy in Post-Taliban Afghanistan", *The Washington Quarterly*, vol. 37, no. 2, Summer 2014; "The Paradox of Iran's Nuclear Consensus", *World Policy Journal*, vol. 26, no. 3, 2009

Khosrow Fatemi, "Leadership By Distrust: The Shah's Modus Operandi", *Middle East Journal*, vol. 36, no. 1, Winter 1982

Leonard Binder, "United States Policy in the Middle East", *Current History*, vol. 84, no. 498, January 1985

Mahmood Sariolghalam, "Transition In The Middle East: New Arab Realities And Iran", *Middle East Policy*, vol. 20, no. 1, Spring 2013

Mark B. Schneider, "Has Iran Covertly Acquired Nuclear Weapons?", *Comparative Strategy*, vol. 32, no. , 2013

Mark N. Katz, "Soviet Policy in the Gulf States", *Current History*, vol. 84, no. 498, January 1985

Masoud Kazemzadeh, Ayatollah Khamenei's Foreign Policy Orientation, *Comparative Strategy*, vol. 32, no. 5, 2013; "Intra-Elite Factionalism and the 2004 Majles Elections in Iran", *Middle Eastern Studies*, vol. 44, no. 2, March 2008

Mathew Kroening, "Time to Attack Iran: Why a Strike Is the Least Bad Option", *Foreign Affairs*, vol. 91, no. 1, January-February 2012

Matteo Legrenzi and Fred H. Lawson, "Iran And Its Neighbours Since 2003: New Dilemmas", *Middle East Policy*, vol. 21, no. 4, Winter 2014

Maziar Behrooz, "Factionalism in Iran under Khomeini", *Middle Eastern Studies*, vol. 27, no. 4, October 1991

Mehran Kamrava, "The 2009 Elections and Iran's Changing Political Landscape", *Orbis*, vol.54, no. 3, Summer 2010; Iranian National-Security Debates: Factionalism And Lost Opportunities, *Middle East Policy*, vol. 14, no. 2, Summer 2007

Mehrdad Madresehee, "The Impact of Oil Price Volatility on Iran's Economy", *Journal of South Asian and Middle Eastern Studies*, vol. 32, no. 3, Spring 2009

Michael A Levi, "Drawing the Line on Iranian Enrichment", *Survival*, vol. 53, no. 4 August September 2011

Mohammad Javad Zarif, "What Iran Really Wants: Iranian Foreign Policy in the Rouhani Era", *Foreign Affairs*, vol. 93, no. 3, May/June 2014

Mohsen M Milani, "Tehran's Take", *Foreign Affairs*, vol. 88, no. 4, July-August 2009; "Is US-Iran Detente Possible?", *Current History*, vol. 112, no. 758, December 2013; "Why Tehran Won't Abandon Assad(ism)", *The Washington Quarterly*, vol. 36, no. 4, Fall 2013

Nader Entessar, "Factional Politics in Post-Khomeini Iran: Domestic and Foreign Policy Implications", *Journal of South Asian and Middle Eastern Studies*, vol. 17, no. 4, Summer 1994

Niv Farago, "Don't Turn Iran into North Korea! Re-Examining Neoconservative Strategy", *Middle East Policy*, vol. 21, no. 3, Fall 2014

Paola Rivetti and Francesco Cavatorta, " 'The Importance of Being Civil Society': Student Politics and the Reformist Movement in Khatami's Iran", *Middle Eastern Studies*, vol. 49, no. 4, 2013

Paul Kerr, "The Atomic Energy Organisation of Iran: What Role?", *Arms Control Today*, vol. 44, no. 8, October 2014

Rashed Uz Zaman, "Strategic Culture: A "Cultural" Understanding of War", *Comparative Strategy*, vol. 28, no. 1, 2009

Ray Takeyh, "Iran:From Reform to Revolution?", *Survival*, vol. 46, no. 1, Spring 2004; "Iran at a Crossroads", *The Middle East Journal*, vol.57, no.1, Winter 2003

R K Ramazani, "Iran's Islamic Revolution and the Persian Gulf", Current History, vol. 84, no. 498, January 1985; "Iran: Burying The Hatchet", *Foreign Policy*, no. 60, Fall 1985; "Who Lost America? The Case of Iran", *Middle East Journal*, vol. 36, no. 1, Winter 1892; "Iran's Foreign Policy: Contending Orientations", *Middle East Journal*, vol. 43, no. 2, Spring 1989

Robert Hewson, "The Sinking Feeling: Iran's Anti-Ship Missile Array", *Rusi Defence Systems*, Summer 2012

Saeid Golkar, "Iran's Revolutionary Guard: Its Views of The United States", *Middle East Policy*, vol. 21, no. 2, Summer 2014

Samir Tata, "Recalibrating American Gran Strategy: Softening US Policies Toward Iran In Order to Contain China", *Parameters*, vol.42, no. 4/vol. 43, no.1, Winter-Spring 2013

Shahram Chubin, "Is Iran a Military Threat?", *Survival*, vol. 56, no. 2, April-May 2014

Shahrough Akhavi, "Elite Factionalism In The Islamic Republic of Iran",

Middle East Journal, vol. 41, no. 2, Spring 1987

Steven R. Ward, "The Continuing Evolution of Iran's Military Doctrine", *Middle East Journal*, vol. 59, no. 4, Autumn 2005

Thomas Juneau, "Iran Under Rouhani: Still Alone In The World", *Middle East Policy*, vol. 21, no. 4, Winter 2014

W. Andrew Terrill, "Iran's Strategy for Saving Asad", *Middle East Journal*, vol. 69, no. 2, Spring 2015

Wyn Bowen and Matthew Moran, "Iran's Nuclear Programme: A Case Study in Hedging?", *Comparative Security Policy*, vol. 35, no. 1, 2014

Zoltan Batany, "Revolt and Resilience in the Arab Kingdoms", *Parameters*, vol. 43, no. 2, Summer 2013

Weekly/Fortnightly Periodicals

- Resalat

- Jane's Defence Weekly

- Hayat-e

Reports

FBIS-MEA (Foreign Broadcasting Information Service-Middle East and Africa

FBIS-NESA (Foreign Broadcasting Information Service-Near East and South Asia)

FBIS-SA (Foreign Broadcasting Information Service-South Asia)

Newspapers

Islamic Republic News Agency (IRNA) (Persian and English)

Mehr News Agency (MNA) (English and Persian)

Fars News Agency (FNA) (English and Persian)

Kayhan Hawai (English and Persian)

Asr Iran

Tehran Times

Iran Times

Financial Times

Index